Teaching with Cases

David Dunne
Kim Brooks

STLHE
SAPES

Society for Teaching and Learning in Higher Education

La société pour l'avancement de la pédagogie dans l'enseignement supérieur

STLHE Green Guides

Series Editors: W. Alan Wright
Université du Québec
UQAR: Campus de Lévis
Lévis, QC G6V 8R9

Eileen Herteis
Purdy Crawford Teaching Centre
Mount Allison University
Sackville, NB E4L 1B7

Christopher Knapper
Instructional Development Centre
Queen's University,
Kingston, ON K7L 3N6

Carol O'Neil
Centre for Learning and Teaching
Dalhousie University
Halifax, NS B3H 4J3

Design: Dalhousie University Graphics

Distributed on behalf of STLHE by:
Dalhousie University Bookstore
University Avenue
Halifax, Nova Scotia B3H 4R2

and

Centre for Learning and Teaching
Dalhousie University
Halifax, Nova Scotia B3H 4R2

Library and Archives Canada Cataloguing in Publication
Dunne, David (1953 -)
     Teaching with cases/David Dunne, Kim Brooks

Includes bibliographical references.
ISBN 0-7703-8924-4

1. College teaching. I. Brooks, Kim II. Society for Teaching and Learning in Higher Education.
III Title.

LB2331.D85 2004   378.1'25   C2004-903704-8

Cite as:
Dunne, David and Brooks, Kim (2004). Teaching with Cases. Halifax, NS: Society for Teaching and
     Learning in Higher Education.

Foreword

The Series Editors are very pleased to present Green Guide Number 5. We are sure that our readers will find *Teaching with Cases* by David Dunne of the University of Toronto and Kim Brooks of the University of British Columbia to be an insightful, informative, and practical Guide to a multi-faceted approach to engaging students in their learning. True to the essence of the STLHE Green Guides, the authors have succeeded in capturing the complexity and many nuances of teaching with cases while avoiding an overemphasis on theory.

Our authors are uniquely qualified to write this guide to teaching with cases due to their particular experiences and professional school perspectives. David Dunne teaches in a prominent business school and has incorporated case teaching in his classroom for many years. Kim Brooks teaches in a well-known law school and draws on her background in this academic field. The authors were supported by Rosamund Woodhouse, of the Queen's University Faculty of Medicine, as she contributed two chapters and invaluable insights into the subject of teaching with cases. The guide strikes a balance by presenting generic uses of teaching with cases while illustrating applications to specific fields.

The Society for Teaching and Learning in Higher Education has sold thousands of Green Guides since Allan J. Gedalof's *Teaching Large Classes* appeared in 1998. Interest in the Green Guides project has increased steadily since then, and we are happy to announce three writing teams are busily preparing Guides 6, 7, and 8.

The STLHE Green Guide series is patterned after the successful publications of our sister organization, HERDSA, in Australasia. Dr. Christopher Knapper was responsible for introducing the idea in Canada and he remains active as a Series Editor. Chris and I are delighted to announce that Carol O'Neil of Dalhousie University and Eileen Herteis of Mount Allison University have joined the editorial team. We invite you to contact us with your criticisms, your accolades, and your suggestions for the future!

Alan Wright
Series Editor
On behalf of
Eileen Herteis
Christopher Knapper
Carol O'Neil

About the Authors

David Dunne

David Dunne teaches marketing, branding and advertising at the Rotman School of Management at the University of Toronto. He has also taught at Queen's University and worked in industry as a marketing manager before completing his Ph.D. in Management at the University of Toronto. Cases figure strongly in his teaching and he has given several workshops on the subjects of case and discussion teaching.

Kim Brooks

After graduating from degree programs at the University of Toronto, University of British Columbia, and Osgoode Hall Law School, Kim Brooks has returned to the University of British Columbia to teach law. She has also taught at Queen's University, and has practiced tax law. Her teaching subjects include tax and torts, and she loves being in the classroom and teaching with cases.

Contents

Acknowledgments

This Green Guide would not have been possible without the invaluable help and advice of many individuals. In particular, Ros Woodhouse, who contributed Chapters 3 and 5, also provided essential expertise in the field of teaching and learning.

We are indebted to anonymous reviewers who gave comments on the manuscript and to Alan Wright, who provided valuable suggestions, encouragement, and help throughout the process of development and publication of the manuscript.

Preface

As case teaching has grown in popularity, so has the need to develop guidelines for practice. Case studies are now used in a wide range of disciplines, from engineering to social science to education. In this Green Guide, we review how cases are used in a variety of fields, with a view to providing readers with principles for effective teaching with cases.

Cases mean different things to different people. The Association for Case Teaching defines the case method as "a means of participatory and dialogical teaching and learning by group discussion of actual events." This definition can encompass written cases, video cases, interactive cases, simulations, games, field trips—but the important elements indicate that case teaching is participatory, discussion-focused, and uses actual events to illustrate general principles. There is no single "case method": even within disciplines, different instructors use cases in very different ways.

Because of the range of case methods, we believe it would be folly to prescribe a single method that is better than the alternatives. Successful case teachers achieve their results in diverse ways, drawing on a wide variety of methods, and their own idiosyncratic styles. We cannot, then, provide a precise definition. Yet cases have many desirable attributes: they foster a highly engaging and involving form of student-centred learning and provide students with the opportunity for practice and reflection. Using case studies, students can become active learners and develop discipline-specific skills, the ability to work effectively with others, and the confidence to think critically and to articulate their views.

In the first three chapters of this Green Guide, we consider how cases are used in our own disciplines—law, business, and medicine. In Chapter 4 we report on the results of an STLHE Listserv survey on member experiences with case teaching. In Chapters 5, 6, and 7, we discuss the basic principles underlying the use of cases as well as their strengths and limitations, and in Chapters 8 to 12 we provide practical guidelines to help instructors develop their own case teaching methodologies. We conclude the Green Guide with sources of cases and further reading on case teaching and learning.

Our intent is to provide a guide that is both useful to case teaching novices and one that provides new ideas to its more experienced practitioners. However, your level of interest in parts of this guide will depend on your own circumstances. We suggest the following:

- If your primary interest is in the variety of ways in which cases are used across disciplines, read Chapters 1 to 4.

- If you are interested in why cases are used, what they can achieve, and some basic principles for teaching with cases, read Chapters 5, 6, and 7.

- If you are interested in the specifics—how to select or write cases, lead a case discussion, assess students, or deal with common problems, read Chapters 8 to 12.

Part 1: The Use of Cases across Disciplines

The purpose of this part of the Green Guide is to describe how case teaching is used in some of the traditional case-based disciplines—law, business, and medicine.

The discussion in each of these sections sets out the origin of the approach, reviews the objectives of the case method, and provides an overview of how the case method is practised. While law, business, and medicine are the disciplines that have relied most heavily on cases, this part of the guide concludes with a section on the use of the case method by STLHE members across a range of disciplines.

1. Law

Origin of the Case Method in Law

Although there is some debate about the originator of the case method in law, its adoption is most often attributed to Christopher Columbus Langdell, a professor at Harvard Law School. In 1870, when Langdell became Dean of Law at Harvard, he promoted this method throughout the school.

Langdell's approach to teaching required both learning the law by exploring judicial decisions (cases), and teaching the law using the Socratic method. Prior to the implementation of the case method, law school was taught primarily through lectures, sometimes supplemented with text. Langdell's vision of the case method differed from this earlier norm in two fundamental ways. First, he believed that law should be taught mainly by providing students with one of the primary sources of law—cases. Second, instead of lecturing the class on the legal rules, Langdell sought to teach students using the Socratic method. Although various instructors employ different versions of what is generally termed the Socratic method, in its truest form the instructor provides no answers to students, but instead guides students through the material with a series of questions. While the case method can be distinguished from the Socratic approach to teaching, in law the two are often practised together.

Although the use of the Socratic method has eroded and instructors in law generally rely on lectures supplemented with questions (sometimes referred to as quasi-Socratic), the case method has proved remarkably resilient. Most law school classes are taught through an analysis of appellate level court decisions. For many courses students purchase casebooks containing edited versions of appeal court decisions and some minor amount of commentary written by the text's author. Although millions of cases are available, a casebook generally excerpts a relatively small number of cases on a given topic such as family law, contract law, company law, or property law.

Why Use Cases in Law

Teachers use cases to achieve different ends in the classroom. However, some objectives of case teaching in law are relatively common. Authors who have explored these objectives in greater detail include Friedland (1996), Garner (2000), and Weaver (1991).

Learn Substantive Law and Legal Process. Most obviously, perhaps, the case method is helpful in law because cases are a primary source of the law. By studying cases, students (1) learn to read and understand case law (in other words, learn how to learn the law); (2) learn some of the substantive law in a particular subject area; and (3) begin to understand something about legal procedure.

Teach Students to "Think Like a Lawyer." Instructors in law could debate for a long time the precise meaning of "thinking like a lawyer." However, there is undoubtedly some common ground. Using the case method, students are expected to learn to sort relevant from irrelevant material, to reconcile seemingly divergent legal and factual positions, to distinguish seemingly similar legal and factual positions, to understand the context and implications of legal decisions, and to make sound arguments on all sides of a particular issue.

Promote Judgement. Anthony Kronman has aptly termed this skill the development of moral imagination (Kronman, 2000). The case method requires students to put themselves into the shoes of each of the parties—the parties to the dispute and the judge or adjudicator. As a result of its demand that students transfer their focus from one party to the next, and that ultimately they train themselves to find a way to judge the merits of each party's claims, the case method "serves as a forcing ground for the moral imagination by cultivating [a] peculiar bifocality" (p. 649).

Enhance Advocacy. Law students inevitably find that advocacy skills are required—whether they end up working as lawyers on behalf of clients, as government agents, or as politicians. It could be argued, in fact, that advocacy skills are necessary regardless of one's ultimate career path.

Questioning students in class, and requiring them to respond based on the materials they read in advance, is intended at least in part to enhance students' advocacy skills. Practice at being 'put on the spot,' and at having your views scrutinized by a professor and peers, is seen to be one of the advantages of the case method approach to teaching.

Develop Critical Analysis. The Socratic method assists students to develop critical analysis. Instructors ask students about all aspects of the context of the legal decision. Queries like "Would this case have been decided the same way if X had occurred instead of Y?" or "What policy concerns underlie the judicial reasoning in this case?" or "Does the reasoning in this case make sense?" are intended to provoke students to think beyond the text of the case.

Example of a Law Case

Most cases assigned in law school classes are appeal level decisions. The following case is significantly shorter than many, but contains the essential elements of any case that might be discussed. That is, the judge who authored the decision has set out a set of facts (what happened), articulated (often inferentially) a problem that needs to be resolved, and has provided a rationale for his or her decision.

GEORGE B. RANSON ET AL.

v.

NATHANIEL KITNER.

31 Ill.App. 241, 1888 WL 2362 (Ill.App. 3 Dist.)

CONGER, J.

This was an action brought by appellee against appellants to recover the value of a dog killed by appellants, and a judgment rendered for $50.

The defense was that appellants were hunting for wolves, that appellee's dog had a striking resemblance to a wolf, that they in good faith believed it to be one, and killed it as such.

Many points are made, and a lengthy argument filed to show that error in the trial below was committed, but we are inclined to think that no material error occurred to the prejudice of appellants.

The jury held them liable for the value of the dog, and we do not see how they could have done otherwise under the evidence. Appellants are clearly liable for the damages caused by their mistake, notwithstanding they were acting in good faith.

We see no reason for interfering with the conclusion reached by the jury, and the judgment will be affirmed.

Judgment affirmed.

Students reading this case would be expected to consider the facts of the case (that one party killed the dog of the second party when they mistook the dog to be a wolf), contemplate the problem the court was asked to resolve (does it matter that the party who killed the dog caused the injury by mistake instead of intentionally), and understand the judge's conclusion on the issue (that when one person kills another's dog, even if by mistake, the person causing the injury will be liable for the consequences of his or her actions).

The Case Method as Practised in Law Schools

As will be reiterated throughout this Green Guide, there are many different ways of using cases in the classroom. However, every teacher at the law school faces many of the same issues using the case method: choosing material, preparing for class, conducting the class, and evaluating student learning.

Choosing Material. For many courses in law, instructors choose among casebooks containing material the authors deemed useful in that subject area. Not infrequently, however, instructors prepare their own course materials, or supplement available casebooks with additional cases they want students to explore.

Cases are chosen for a variety of purposes. Some are chosen because they reflect what is perceived to be the current state of the law. In other words, they are the most recent and most authoritative cases on sub-topics within the broader area of law. For example, a recent Supreme Court of Canada case on the liability of municipalities will almost certainly be included in tort law casebooks in the chapter on the liability of public bodies when they cause injuries to others. If the casebook was published prior to the release of this highly authoritative case, an instructor may well include the case in supplemental material.

There are, however, innumerable reasons instructors choose to include certain cases in their reading material. For example, even though some cases do not reflect the current state of the law, they raise issues or present reasoning interesting enough that instructors feel their students should read and understand the decision. Similarly, instructors may choose a series of cases that reveal the development of judicial thinking. Further, some cases might be included because they are perceived to be part of the legal canon. To illustrate, all lawyers might be familiar with the decision of *Donoghue v. Stephenson* (1932), the case thought to be the main source of modern negligence law, even though the law of negligence has developed significantly since that time. In addition, instructors may include cases to demonstrate trends in the decision-making of particular judges, because the facts in the case are compelling, or because the issue in the case is contentious.

Perhaps surprisingly, instructors and casebook authors often include a case because they disagree with the reasoning or outcome of the case. Instructors may use such a case to reveal flaws in judicial reasoning or to demonstrate biases reflected in the decision. For example, an instructor may choose a case that denies women the right to own property as a mechanism for raising a discussion of the effect of social context and judicial attitudes on what might otherwise be seen as the impartial nature of judges.

At the Start of the Course. It is useful for the instructor to provide a clear sense of the course's direction in the first class. Particularly in the first year of law school, students need at least some direction to orient themselves to the nature of the course, the kind of material that will be covered, the pace of the classes, and the instructor's expectations for their participation and evaluation.

Preparing for Class. It is imperative that both students and instructors be well prepared for class for the case method to work effectively. Students are urged to prepare briefs, including a short summary of the facts of the case, an attempt to articulate the issue under review, a discussion of the court's reasoning, and a statement of the dispute's resolution. Students are then able to use these notes as a reference point for the discussion to take place in the classroom.

An instructor who intends to employ the Socratic method of questioning, even in conjunction with a lecture, must understand the details of the decision and thoroughly consider the implications of and ambiguities in the decision. In Canada, most casebooks do not have instructors' solutions, so instructors often meet with others who teach in the same area to ensure that they fully understand cases and are able to direct students though the discussion of the case. After gaining a thorough grasp of the case under review, most instructors simply map out the questions they will pose in their notes; however, other methods are also available. Some instructors may use PowerPoint or other technologies to move students from one topic, issue, or question to the next. Some instructors ask students to prepare and submit questions that might be posed to the other students in the class before the class begins, or provide questions for consideration to students in advance of the class.

Conducting the Class. Case method classes in law range from lecture format to close to full Socratic method, where the instructor discloses no information and simply asks questions. The less structured the discussion, the more important it is for the instructor to exercise judgement in questioning students to prevent the discussion from becoming completely sidetracked. Students may provide a multitude of different answers to a question posed by an instructor, and the instructor must be prepared to respond to the course of the dialogue.

The most conventional approach begins the discussion of a case with relatively simple questions, posed by the instructor and answered by the students. What happened? Who was involved? What did the court have to decide? What was the outcome? More complicated questions can follow when the class is warmed up. Why did the judge or judges decide the way they did? Does this case seem consistent with other cases that have been discussed in the course? What do you think would happen if one of the facts were different?

Evaluating Student Learning. Most law school classes are evaluated by 100% final examination (Kissam, 2001). Exams are usually time-limited and based on hypothetical fact patterns that students are expected to analyze. It is relatively common for students to be graded on a curve in assessing performance on exams. Many instructors in law acknowledge that this situation is not desirable, and that it fails to emphasize one of the most important skills for lawyers—writing. However, increasing class sizes, the general absence in law of teaching assistants, and the demands of employers have resulted in the continued adoption of high-stakes final exams.

2. Business

Origin of the Case Method in Business

The roots of case teaching in business trace back to the birth of the Harvard Business School (HBS) in 1908. The school's first Dean, Edwin F. Gay, embraced the case method in response to its success at the Harvard Law School. Dean Gay's successor, Wallace B. Donham, encouraged faculty to collect cases and by 1924 most courses at HBS used cases as their primary method of instruction.

The Harvard tradition of case teaching is based on the philosophy that students learn best when exposed to managerial problems demanding thinking and the application of managerial principles. The situations portrayed are typically multidimensional and ambiguous, and students must make tradeoffs between conflicting influences. In discussing the case with others, individuals are forced to confront their own assumptions and values.

Proponents of the case method argue that learning is anchored in reality and based on experience. As a result, students tend to retain knowledge and achieve understanding more effectively using the case method than through lectures. The student's own experience, and that of other students, dominates the learning process and, consequently, the learning experience can be very powerful.

The case method has spread widely to other business schools, although Harvard remains the most committed to it, reporting that 80% of its teaching is by the case method. According to *Business Week*, the top 30 schools in the US, excluding Harvard, used cases an average of 37% of the time in 2002. In Canada, the Ivey Business School at the University of Western Ontario models itself on Harvard and uses cases 70% of the time.

Why Use Cases in Business

Cases are a form of experiential learning in which students are encouraged to (sometimes literally) play the role of a manager facing a challenging decision. They call for *inductive reasoning* in that their purpose is to derive general principles from a specific situation. They are used in a wide variety of courses and learning situations. The following are some of their more common goals:

Develop Analytical Skills. Business cases typically provide both quantitative and qualitative information related to the problem. Students are required to select information to analyze, to apply appropriate analytical tools, and to interpret the results correctly.

Develop Sound Business Judgement. Students are expected to synthesize and evaluate the facts and arguments presented to them in the case to arrive at balanced and appropriate decisions.

Test Understanding and Application of Theory. Theoretical readings are often assigned with cases in the expectation that students will use the readings to shed light on the case; alternatively, the instructor may introduce theory at an appropriate point in the class discussion. Students' attempts to apply elements of theory to the facts of the particular case under review can help them decide whether they really understand the theoretical concepts.

Provide a Real-World Perspective. Cases can allow students to see how managerial concepts can be applied to real business situations, and to evaluate the practical usefulness of these concepts.

Motivate a Topic. A case can be used as a means of developing students' appreciation for a type of managerial problem, and tools for solving it can be introduced in class. In this situation, students are expected to prepare the case using concepts learned in the course, and the class discussion takes the process a stage further. In the case "Compaq Computer— Intel Inside?"[1], for example, students are exposed to a set of conditions that defy most market research techniques but are ideally suited to a particular methodology—conjoint analysis. When students come to class, they will have considered these conditions and will be interested in hearing about a new technique that solves the problem.

Engage and Involve Students. Cases can be a powerful way of engaging students. Because these are real-world problems, they appeal to the practical focus of most business students. In addition, the process of solving a problem by placing oneself in a decision-maker's shoes can be much more engaging than an abstract lecture.

Learn to Work in Groups. Case work typically involves solitary preparation, work in small groups, and discussion in class. Both small-group work and class discussion challenge students by exposing them to world views and fields of experience other than their own.

Develop Self-Confidence. Confidence in one's own judgement is an important quality for managers. Students develop personal confidence through the case method by learning the value of their knowledge in solving problems and by exposing their ideas to the constructive scrutiny of others.

Develop Presentation Skills. For some students, presentations in front of a group can be especially challenging. Case work in business schools often involves presentation to the class and can develop students' confidence and skills in this area.

On the other hand, there are some situations for which cases are not appropriate. Cases are not particularly efficient vehicles for the transmission of knowledge or techniques. While they are intended to simulate real-world situations, they do not replicate reality. Cases are

---

[1] Harvard Business School Case #9-599-061

usually considerably more 'tidy' than the problems managers face in the real world, in which information is often not coherently presented or even available: while the case approach allows students to explore problems in depth, it does sacrifice some realism.

Example of a Business Case

Business cases range from the relatively simple to the very complex. They may be provided in many forms: written, video, interactive, or a combination of these.

The *Crescent School Summer Camps* case is provided here as an example to give readers a sense of the scope of a business case. This case tends towards the simple end of the spectrum and describes a situation faced by two MBA students as they worked on a project for a private boys' school in Toronto. While the full case is too long to reproduce here, the following is an abstract:

> In January, 2002, Crescent School engaged the support of Wendy Chong and Jamie Stiff, MBA students at the Rotman School of Management, to investigate a summer camp for the school, to be launched in 2003. A summer camp was part of headmaster Geoff Roberts' vision for Crescent. It could be a vehicle to enhance the school's relationship with the Greater Toronto community, and, in addition, generate incremental revenue through the usage of facilities that currently lay dormant in the summer. Roberts' vision for the new summer programs would involve a structured, well-organized approach, laying the foundation for a successful offering for years to come. To achieve this, decisions needed to be made on whether summer programs were a viable idea, and, if so, what specific shape such programs would take. Jamie and Wendy were asked to make recommendations to the Board of Crescent School on these issues by mid-April.

The full case provides qualitative and quantitative information on the history and management of Crescent School, the summer camp "industry," Crescent's competitors in the Toronto area and market research conducted by the two MBA students. The full case can be downloaded free of charge at http://www.rotman.utoronto.ca/bicpapers/case/2002.htm

The case exposes some of the tradeoffs involved in developing a market research project. With hindsight, the research conducted by the two MBA students featured in the case was not perfect, and students in the class are encouraged to come up with realistic ways in which they might have improved on it. The fact that the main players in this particular case are students like themselves helps students identify with them and tends to bring the situation alive.

The Case Method as Practised in Business Schools

As noted earlier, in practice there is a wide variety of methods of teaching with cases. Common elements are selection of appropriate materials, preparation, and discussion. However, individual instructors have developed their own styles and many creative techniques to help students learn. The following guidelines, intended for those new to case teaching, are synthesized from Applegate (1988), Corey (1998), and Erskine, Leenders and Mauffette-Leenders (1998).

Choosing Material. While students are responsible for their own learning in a case course, the instructor exerts a powerful influence through the cases and readings she or he selects. Beyond the specific topics covered, the instructor should take into account the level of difficulty of the cases, how they are sequenced, and how students have responded to them in the past. To help with this, the instructor can keep notes on the class discussion each time a case is used.

At the Start of the Course. It is useful to establish standards of preparation and classroom behaviour at the start of the course. By having a complete grasp of the first case and by challenging inaccurate assertions, the instructor can indicate to students that they are responsible for knowing the facts of the case in future discussions.

In addition, the instructor can model the importance of respectful listening by showing tolerance for different points of view and by asking students to comment on each other's statements.

Preparing for Class. Students are expected to prepare the case thoroughly for class, individually and in groups. Mauffette-Leenders, Erskine, and Leenders (1997) propose a "3-Stage Learning Process" in which students first prepare individually, then in small groups, then discuss the case in class. Instructors should thoroughly prepare the case and the case discussion process: how it will begin, what avenues it may follow, and how it should end. Cases are often supplied with teaching notes, in which the case's author comments on issues raised and suggested teaching methods; case teachers, however, often prefer to conduct their own analysis and discussion planning based on their understanding of their students' needs.

There is a balance between being structured enough to achieve the learning goals of the session, and flexible enough to pursue valuable avenues that arise from the students' experience. Many instructors develop a board plan, a physical representation of how the chalkboard should look by the end of class; this highlights major themes but is flexible enough to build in students' perspectives. Some instructors also plan mini-lectures into a case session, to be delivered at appropriate points in the discussion.

Class Discussion.

Beginning of class. The instructor usually introduces the case by summarizing the situation facing the decision-maker. She or he may also comment on the issues raised by the case and their importance to managers; the intent of this is to create an air of anticipation and to increase interest in the topic, but not to pre-empt the discussion. Before the class discussion begins, a student may be selected to open the discussion; while the student will have read and analyzed the case in advance, usually she or he is given a few minutes to prepare opening comments.

During class. Following the initial student presentation, the instructor typically invites comments from other students. At this stage, the instructor is not too directive but may ask students for clarification and justification of their ideas, listing comments on the chalkboard, relating comments to each other, and bringing some order to the discussion. The objective in this phase of the discussion is to involve as many students as possible and to bring out the major issues. The instructor then may ask for further discussion on each of several broad areas. Throughout the discussion, the instructor strikes a delicate balance between leading students to probe deeply into the issues of the case and risking demotivating them by being too directive.

End of class. The end of a case class usually consists of a summary of the case discussion and an assessment of what has been learned. The instructor manages the discussion so as to leave time for an effective ending. Some instructors choose to provide a summary themselves, in the form of a mini-lecture outlining the principles underlying the case or informal feedback to the class; others ask a student to summarize the discussion and its broader lessons.

After class. Instructors often stay after class to address questions that may remain in some students' minds. Students are often evaluated on their class participation (at some schools this can account for 50% of their total grade); instructors may take a few minutes after class to record individuals' participation while it is fresh in their minds. This is also a good opportunity to write some notes on the case and the class response for future reference.

3. Medicine

Origin of the Case Method in Medicine

Much contemporary writing about teaching with cases in medical education conveys the impression that this is a recent innovation, synonymous with problem-based learning. However, the use of cases in medical teaching is probably as old and as varied as medicine itself. Treatises from the time of Hippocrates describe medical cases for teaching and reference purposes, writers in the early medical journals described cases to teach other physicians about new conditions and treatments, and the tradition of teaching and communicating about medical cases continues to the present day[2]. A search of currMIT (the North American database for undergraduate medical school curriculum information and management) for scheduled teaching sessions that use case methods identified over 3000 sessions listed by

---

[2] We are grateful to Jackie Duffin, a medical historian, who confirmed the history and suggested the sources.

participating medical schools. This number excludes the countless numbers of real cases that students encounter and learn from during clinical phases of their training.

Why Use Cases in Medicine

Some common goals underlie using cases:

Increase Motivation for Learning. Teaching with clinical cases shows the relevance of fundamental scientific knowledge for medical practice, and so increases the desire to learn.

Structure Knowledge in Ways that Can Be Used in Clinical Contexts. Students must transform information into knowledge they can use in medical practice. Experience with cases helps connect the factual information (lists of symptoms, medical findings, etc.) that students read with how the symptoms actually appear in a patient or on a medical report, and provides opportunities to connect underlying theories with clinical manifestations.

Promote Integration of Knowledge. Clinical cases can involve multiple issues and domains of knowledge or skill. Learners must be aware of all these aspects and be able to integrate them effectively in order to understand a clinical problem. For example, a case describing a situation where parents request genetic counseling about the risk of a hereditary disease in their unborn child would require integration of biomedical, psycho-social, legal, and ethical issues.

Develop Clinical Reasoning Skills. Cases can be discussed at critical junctures that require clinical reasoning to make decisions. A description of the initial signs and symptoms in a case provides an opportunity to practise formulating hypotheses about potential diagnoses and determining further investigations. New information yielded by investigations can lead to refinement of these strategies and decisions about how the case is to be managed in the future.

Develop Self-Directed Learning Skills. The rapid rate of change in medical knowledge has resulted in widespread agreement that self-directed learning is an essential skill for physicians. Part of the rationale for case teaching methods is to help physicians routinely identify their own learning needs and address them independently. Hence, in problem-based learning, learners start by examining the case to determine what they need to learn, and then use varied resources to acquire that knowledge.

Promote Evidence-Based Practice. A fundamental concern of contemporary medicine is that practice is grounded on evidence of effectiveness. In advanced levels of medical education, knowledge gaps identified in dealing with a case are intended to prompt students to search for evidence on the issue.

Example of a Medicine Case

Cases used in medical teaching typically start with a description of basic information about a patient and the situation that has led them to seek medical attention. Additional information about the history of the present illness and results of investigations set the stage for students to identify relevant issues for reaching a diagnosis or management plan. The following example is used in teaching principles of palliative care to undergraduate medical students:[3]

> Mr. Bruce is a 78-year-old patient that you have known for many years. He has long standing chronic obstructive pulmonary disease (COPD) with increasing numbers of admissions to the acute care hospital over the past year for exacerbations usually associated with pneumonia. With each episode, Bruce tells you to "fix him up" so that he can get back to his hobbies of fishing and woodcarving. A retired military officer, he tends to be gruff at times and treasures his solitude and independence. Mr. Bruce is a widower with four children who are supportive, but live from Vancouver to Halifax. One son, Peter lives locally but has teenage children and a business to run. He looks in on his dad about once a week.
>
> Mr. Bruce has become increasingly debilitated by dyspnea over the past few months, and his son has called your office today expressing concerns about his dad's ability to manage on his own. From previous discussions with Mr. Bruce, you are aware that he is adamant about staying in his own home.
>
> Present medications are:
>
> Ventolin inhaler ii puffs q4h prn
>
> Atrovent inhaler 1v puffs q4h
>
> Milk of magnesia 30 cc prn

The case integrates issues such as the definition of palliative care, symptom management and treatment options, goals and settings for care, and family concerns. It is used to challenge students to construct a management strategy that incorporates these elements appropriately.

Case Methods as Practised in Medicine

Medical teaching uses cases in a variety of ways, according to the learning objectives and the settings in which learning is taking place. Pre-clinical education, the earliest phase of medical education, is largely classroom-based, and emphasizes building knowledge required for subsequent clinical work. While cases are also used in subsequent clinical education, our focus here is on their use in classroom settings.

---

[3] We are grateful to Corinne Schroder who generously allowed us to include this case.

Initial courses establish a foundation of basic scientific knowledge (biochemistry, physiology, anatomy, etc.), and connect this knowledge to systems in the human body and related disorders. The predominant instructional approaches used during the preclinical phase of medical education are lectures and problem-based learning. Both incorporate cases, but use them for different purposes and in different ways. In addition, cases are used in both teaching and assessing clinical skills. These varying approaches are discussed below.

Lectures and Seminars. In case-based lectures, case discussion can be used for several purposes:

- to raise interest in topics or establish their relevance
- to convey information
- to teach the cognitive skills required to gather and interpret information to formulate diagnoses and treatment plans (clinical reasoning)
- to assess students' knowledge

An especially interesting case might be described early in a lecture to stimulate curiosity about a topic or to demonstrate the clinical relevance of underlying scientific principles. Short cases accompanied by questions can also be used early in class as a form of needs assessment or to review material if they are used at the end of a session. For example, the case described above could be adapted in the following ways. It could be used for a needs assessment with questions to determine whether learners were familiar with the issues. It could be used for review by accompanying it with questions focused on particular aspects or with the task of preparing a management strategy.

In a 'running case,' information about a case might be used sequentially to provide a structure for each session. Discussion of the case could both convey information and involve students in problem solving. For example, a class might start with an account of a telephone call between an emergency physician and a medical specialist, relating information about a patient who had arrived with a particular set of symptoms. Initial discussion might focus on developing hypotheses about the cause of the symptoms and the further information the specialist would look for if he or she were to interview the patient or conduct further investigations. The actual diagnosis could then be used to generate further discussion—about the process of reaching such a decision or about how a particular management plan would be decided. 'What if' questions could be used at any point to probe issues that had been missed or to initiate new areas for discussion.[4]

Other approaches use several very short cases. A series of similar cases can be used to demonstrate how the presentation of a condition might vary across patients or in particular circumstances. Brief discussions about a series of different cases can be used to enhance

---

[4] We are grateful to Mark Goldszmidt for this example.

learning about of a range of conditions. For example, Chew (2001) described positive outcomes with an approach in which learners were presented with multiple cases (radiograph images) and asked to write a best diagnosis or short differential diagnosis for each image. Learners then took turns discussing their responses to the images.

Problem-Based Learning. Pressure to adopt more active methods for learning in medicine and to foster self-directed learning has led to widespread adoption of problem-based learning (PBL), a method based on cases.

The primary purposes of PBL cases are to stimulate learning and to prepare students to learn in a self-directed way later in their careers. Structuring activities around cases provides a way to contextualize information, and the combination of self-direction and social interaction in PBL can enhance the quality of the learning experience.

A PBL case typically describes the initial presentation, subsequent tests, and progress of a patient. In addition, PBL cases often include information that raises ethical, psychosocial, or other issues relevant to understanding health, illness, and the role of the physician. Usually the case is distributed in written format, although video clips have been used in some institutions.

The PBL process follows a cycle of small group discussion and self-directed learning. In the first phase, a small group of students (led by a tutor who facilitates the group process) is presented with a description of a patient and the circumstances that have led the person to seek medical attention. The case is read aloud, and discussion is used to construct an understanding of the case, to identify points the students need to know more about, and to form hypotheses. These become learning objectives for independent study, to be discussed at the next session. The cycle may have two or more iterations that introduce more information about the patient's condition, results of investigations, and other factors that might enter the situation.

Although the term 'PBL' is often used as if it referred to a single method, there are many variations in the way it is implemented. For example, learning objectives for cases may be determined entirely by students or directed by an 'official' list. Other variations emphasize the skills and process of working in a group.

Team Learning. Team Learning (TL) is a structured method for using cases that has been introduced recently into medicine from business and science (Searle *et al.*, 2003). Like PBL, it involves students in small group discussions, but with the practical advantage that it does not require a faculty tutor for each group and so is significantly less resource-intensive. TL can be used within a single session (it may be especially helpful in review sessions) or section of a course, or for entire courses.

Team Learning follows a repeating cycle of three phases. The first phase requires learners to study assigned materials independently. The materials are focused on clearly identified objectives, which students are then tested on in an individual multiple choice exam in Phase 2. Students then work in small groups during class time and submit their consensus answers for immediate scoring and discussion by the whole class. In Phase 3 the groups use the knowledge gained during the earlier phases to discuss cases that require application and problem solving. Again all groups share and discuss their answers with the whole class.

Proponents of TL argue that the use of individual and group tests, comparisons of group responses and discussions enhances learning by increasing accountability for adequate preparation, providing feedback, and consolidating understanding. Proponents also argue that TL enables more effective incentives for group interaction and effective teamwork than PBL or traditional instructional methods.

Teaching Clinical Skills. While PBL is well suited for knowledge acquisition and integration, medical education must also address the interpersonal and clinical skills required to work with patients. These include skills in taking an appropriate medical history, communicating a diagnosis, and negotiating a treatment plan with a patient. An important method of achieving this is by practising cases with community or patient volunteers, or with actors (known as standardized patients) who have been trained to simulate particular conditions and to give feedback on the process of the encounter.

Assessing Clinical Skills. 'Real time' simulated cases are also used in formal assessments of clinical skills and knowledge. In these exams, known as Objective Structured Clinical Exams (or OSCEs), students are assessed on their performance across a series of short case scenarios. Each case is designed to assess the ability of the student to perform tasks such as taking a case history, performing a physical examination, formulating a diagnosis, and planning a course of action.

4. How STLHE Members Use Cases

An author's post to the STLHE ListServ (see Appendix 1) on October 29, 2003 requested information about subscribers' use of cases. The 11 responses received, representing eight different disciplines and professional fields, are summarized in this chapter.

The size and scope of the responses varied from brief suggestions for case teaching based on personal experience to several pages of discussion and references.

The major themes are discussed below and highlighted by quotations from respondents. Since this is not a scientific sample, our approach has been to develop a reasonably coherent narrative based on respondents' comments rather than to provide a definitive summary.

Selecting Cases

Some respondents wrote their own cases, while others selected them from existing sources. Linda provided a useful summary of the key factors involved in the selection of cases:

[Cases should be:]

- Tied tightly to course material & objectives
- Have realistic & relevant plots for today—enhanced by drama/suspense, technical detail, empathetic character development, and dialogue
- Have general applicability
- Contain relevant and irrelevant information
- Present a dilemma with multiple uncertain, risky, &/or controversial solutions

Linda, Faculty Development

Respondents selected cases based on their **objectives** for both the course and the session. These were set at the beginning of the course and cases were selected in anticipation of students' learning as the course progresses:

I plan my course or workshop by developing an overall conceptual model or framework and based on underlying theory. First I set topics and their sequence, then establish learning objectives. After this I can then identify which topics require cases and how many cases I need for the whole course or workshop.

Aldene, Business

Beyond course objectives, faculty had a variety of other criteria in mind in case selection. One dimension was the level of **difficulty** of the case. A specific tool for case selection was the "Case Difficulty Cube" proposed by Maufette-Leenders, Erskine, and Leenders (1997), which provides a scoring system for cases on three aspects of difficulty: analytical, conceptual and presentation. The course would begin with "easy" cases on all three dimensions and more difficult cases were introduced as the course progressed. This idea is discussed further in Chapter 8.

A further basis for case selection was **realism**. Several respondents noted the need for cases to be realistic or based on real-world experience:

The case study should be . . . filled with enough relevant (and sometimes irrelevant) information to make it "real lif.e"

Catherine, Educational Psychology

Some respondents also suggested that cases should be **concise** (possible to read in 15 minutes) and, over the duration of a course, should **cover a range of practical contexts**:

We seek cases in all practice milieux, portraying clients of all ages, with all sorts of diagnoses. This is because all may be encountered in practice, and thus to be comprehensive, the education must cover all of these.

Sandra, Occupational Therapy

While concise, cases should also be sufficiently **rich** to provide students with issues to discuss. There should be no single right answer; moreover, there should be some irrelevant information to develop students' judgement about what is important:

What makes a good case? Well, for me, it has to be complex enough to not offer an immediate solution. I also like to find cases that have no clear "right" solution or answer. I want the students to disagree, discuss, debate the issues.

Catherine, Educational Psychology

Preparing for Case Teaching

Faculty who teach with cases emphasize the importance of preparation. This includes both communicating expectations to students and preparing oneself for class.

Several respondents mentioned the importance of setting appropriate expectations early in the course. Students who are not accustomed to cases can find it difficult to adapt to the more participative model of case learning. It is important to provide them with guidance early on:

At the start of the curriculum, we talk to the students about respectful diagreement and being safe to express one's opinion or ask questions. I invite shy students to come see me privately for tips/strategies.

Sandra, Occupational Therapy

Aldene provided extensive information on her approach to preparing for a case class, and her comments are summarized below. Preparing students for case learning can involve extensive discussion and exercises in the first class:

The syllabus and introduction are very important. I lay out the whole journey, the conceptual framework, and how their performance will be evaluated.

- Have students complete a description for me of themselves, their interests, and their learning styles at the first class.
- Use name cards and photos so I know who they are.
- Provide the seating plan with the names so they also know who the other students are.

- Give time in the first class for students to introduce themselves in groups of 3, 6. I find even in the 4th year classes, this may be the first time they have actually gotten to know their classmates.
- Have students complete a bio and publish it for sharing on our class website.
- As they participate, I thank them by name for their participation and comments. If they have not volunteered, I invite them directly into the discussion. I note their participation on the seating plan during/after each class.

. Aldene, Business

Preparing oneself for a case class involves both preparation of "content" (the case itself) and "process" (how it will be taught). For Aldene, preparation takes 3-4 times the amount of class time and involves reading the case thoroughly several times, doing the analysis oneself, picking out what is vital and planning the flow of discussion.

Stimulating Discussion

In case classes, it can be important to begin the discussion with an overview of the case. This reminds students of the key facts and allows the instructor an opportunity to start the discussion off in a direction she or he considers fruitful:

Setting it up is important, and I'm learning to do a better job here. It helps to give students an overview, without giving the case away, before you send them off to role play the case. It also helps to focus them on the objectives you are trying to teach.

Susan, Negotiation and Conflict Management

Respondents had a wide range of suggestions for stimulating discussion in case classes. Some of these were very creative and could have applications in any discussion-based class. The variety of responses serves to illustrate the fact that there is no single "case method" but that case teaching leaves the professor with a great deal of scope for innovation. Some of these suggestions are given below.

My favourite method in teaching full cases is to provide a brief summary to students and refer them to sources to research the information and invite students to present the case in class (teach to learn method). I allow 2 students, not more, to do a full class (50 minutes) presentation of the case. This work is assessed as a replacement mark for a written project.

Gabor, Hospitality Management

One of my favourite cases . . . was a committee making a recruitment/selection decision. There are actually 5 different copies of the same case with different pieces of information in each. The case when handed out visually appears the same for everyone. The group is into the middle of the discussion before they suddenly realize that they do not have the same information. (And that is what happens in real life.)

Aldene, Business

I have each group/pair report on certain things on a flipchart and post. We all look at these postings and make observations of similarities and differences. I would begin the discussion with a question directed towards a point/objective that I want to illuminate. I find posting on a flipchart rather than a report from each group keeps the energy level high.

Susan, Negotiation and Conflict Management

Assessing Student Learning

Respondents used a variety of methods, both oral and written, to assess what students had learned from their case courses. Linda suggested some general criteria for assessment on written and oral assignments:

- Reasonable and complex problem definition
- Relevant known info identified
- Relevant unknowns identified
- Relevant unknowns supplied
- Strong rationale for proposed solution
- Limitations of proposed solution identified

Linda, Faculty Development

It is important to establish clear, consistent criteria. These could be established in collaboration with students:

Last semester, while teaching a graduate business class which used cases quite a bit, I once again bemoaned the students' writing skills. I finally decided to work with the students to develop a rubric to evaluate their written case analyses. It led to some interesting class discussions and finally, clear, shared expectations about how I was going to grade their writing.

Tim, Business

However, some respondents indicated that class participation should be assessed in addition to student performance in written and oral assignments. Participation was seen as a way of getting students to support each other's learning rather than a competitive struggle for "airtime." Grades were based on a combination of self-rating by students and the instructor's assessment:

In class, I have used contribution marks. This is not just for opening your mouth and saying something, anything. The VALUE of the contribution is graded. For example, sharing a citation is more valued than expressing an opinion, which is more valued than repeating a fact from the case. I also value more highly sharing clinical experiences, asking questions, pointing out contradictions or agreements, raising overlooked topics, and synthesizing discussion to date. I often use a self rating for part of the contribution mark and as a means of discussion with each student each class.

Sandra, Occupational Therapy

Assessment was also seen as a component of an important "feedback loop" that both allowed students to evaluate their own learning and fill in gaps, and provided the instructor with information she could use in future classes:

I ask students to tell me the lessons they learned. Then I'll have an overhead prepared of the points I wanted them to get. This helps to clarify any misunderstanding around a point and gives them an opportunity to add new findings. This is a cumulative process. Every time a case is used, students make new links/insights, and then I add this to my notes for next time.

Susan, Negotiation and Conflict Management

Dealing with Problems

Several respondents cited students' insufficient preparation for class discussion as a problem in case teaching. To deal with this, respondents used incentives such as grades for participation, and made it clear that good preparation was a prerequisite for effective participation. They approached individual students who were not participating to encourage them to speak up in class.

However, in some instances it became clear to instructors that the class as a whole was not prepared for the discussion. Sandra's comment on class preparation illustrates how destructive the failure to prepare can be and how difficult it is to deal with:

In one memorable (and not in a good way) class, not one student had prepared. The case presented raw assessment data that they had to score and interpret to plan the treatment. I caught on early, because I asked them the score on the assessment and its implications before we proceeded to treatment plan discussion. Not one student knew the score. I did NOT handle it well. I complained and fragged them through the class, but I knew it was a disaster and so did they.

Sandra, Occupational Therapy

Aldene provided some specific suggestions for dealing with the problem of inadequate preparation by the class as a whole:

One way to deal with poor preparation is to turn my back to the class and ask one student to count how many have prepared for the class. They then tell me. I explain that the class has let down their colleagues. On another occasion, I have stopped the case discussion and said it is not worth our while to continue and have left the classroom. (I don't like to do this as I feel it is a bit like a temper tantrum.)

Aldene, Business

Encouraging students to see the general learning that arises from a specific case can also be tricky:

My current main challenge is asking for the right points on the flipchart and then asking the right questions for the most valuable "ah ha's" during the debriefing. I believe the debriefing should add to the learning, not just rehash what happened.

Susan, Negotiation and Conflict Management

As noted earlier, one respondent addressed this issue by asking students for the main points they learned, comparing them with her own learning goals for the class, and using the students' points as input to future sessions on the same topic.

Conclusions

Respondents selected cases based on their compatibility with curriculum, course and session objectives, their level of difficulty, realism, conciseness, their ability to cover a range of contexts, and their potential for rich discussions in class.

Preparation for case classes involved communicating expectations to students early in the course, getting to know the students, and encouraging them to participate. To prepare a case class, instructors work both to understand and analyze the case itself and to prepare the flow of discussion.

Respondents provided several creative ideas on how to stimulate discussion in a case class. Assessment involved not only evaluating students' written and oral work, but also their contribution to the class as a learning community.

The respondents' major problem was insufficient preparation by students. It was important to be sufficiently assertive to make expectations clear to students without going overboard and alienating them.

Part 2: Learning Principles Underlying Case Teaching

The preceding chapters have illustrated the rich variety of goals and strategies for the use of cases in teaching. We intend the next three chapters to provide a brief overview of the theoretical rationale for employing the case method. These chapters provide some of the reasons for using cases, explore some of the strengths and limits of teaching with cases, and outline some principles for the effective use of cases.

5. Principles Underlying Case Teaching

The purpose of this section of the guide is to look at the pedagogical principles that underlie effective teaching with cases. We will discuss the broader rationale for teaching with cases and the common goals that emerge from the descriptions in the earlier Chapters.

Why Teach with Cases? Pedagogical Rationales

Experience and Learning. One of the earliest theoretical rationales for teaching with cases was provided by the influential educational theorist, John Dewey. He argued in 1915 that ". . . education is not an affair of 'telling' and being told, but an active and constructive process" that requires "direct and continuous occupations with things." Further, for these occupations (or experiences) to be educational, they required reflection to transform them into knowledge.

The link between experience, reflection, and learning has been maintained and elaborated by more recent adult education theorists such as Mezirow and Kolb. Kolb's well-known model of experiential learning suggests that an experience can be transformed into knowledge only if it involves reflection, active manipulation, or experimentation. Kreber (2001) argues that the concrete events described in cases facilitate learning because they provide a source of experience for learners, which can then be transformed into learning through reflection or experimentation.

Deep Learning. A significant body of research shows that high quality learning (i.e., learning that is durable and can be applied with flexibility) is dependent on the cognitive processes used during learning. Passive, rote-learning processes, such as memorizing facts, tend to yield poor comprehension and recall. In contrast, 'deep' learning processes actively require learners to 'use' concepts, to link them to prior knowledge, or to apply them to problems. The payoff is improved comprehension and recall. Teaching with cases favours deep learning because it demands such involvement of the learner.

Context-Based Learning. While other teaching methods can also be used to elicit deep processing, an added benefit is that cases provide a context for abstract material.

When abstract materials are taught in the absence of context (for example, if basic scientific principles are taught without linkages to clinical situations), it can be almost impossible for learners to see the connection between the theory and the example. Medical students may fail to recognize characteristic features of medical conditions in real life if they have studied them only in a black and white photograph.

Complex Skill Sets. Complex skills such as problem solving, critical thinking, and clinical reasoning cannot be learned independently of the situations or cases that require their use.

Self-Direction. Finally, theories about self-directed learning offer another justification for the use of cases. Barrows (1985) refers to "closed loop" or "reiterative" learning with cases, whereby learners engage in reflection on changes in their understanding of the initial problem and of the learning resources they have used. The capacity to be a self-directed learner depends in large part on the understanding of one's own learning that results from such reflection. Self-direction has been widely recognized as essential for lifelong, lifewide learning (e.g., Knapper & Cropley, 1991). If cases can be used to stimulate learners to reflect on their own experiences, and to become more effective in their independent learning, then the approach can be very powerful.

Common Goals for Teaching with Cases

Develop Professional Skills. Lynn (1999) has described the general purpose of teaching with cases as furthering "the development of professional intellectual and behavioural skills" (p.3). Many of the goals listed in the earlier chapters fit within this generalization. For example, critical analysis and appraisal, professional judgement, "thinking like a lawyer," and clinical reasoning are among the professional intellectual skills identified prominently in law, business, and medicine. Professionally relevant communications skills are also prominent in the form of advocacy (law), presentation skills (business), and clinical communication skills (medicine).

Develop Self-Directed Learning. While the commonalities of goals across disciplines are clear, there are some interesting differences that reflect the nature and priorities of the different professions. For example, the development of self-directed learning and critical appraisal skills is more prominent in medicine, reflecting the explosive growth of medical research and the ensuing challenge of keeping up with this new knowledge. Goals such as stimulating reflection are more prominent in fields such as education, where critical analysis of personal experience is seen as a central mechanism for professional development (e.g., Kleinfeld, 1992, Shulman, J.H., 1992).

Emphasize Theory. Merseth (1994) considers cases as exemplars to support the development of prepositional knowledge and to emphasize the role of theory. The goals reported in the earlier chapters are consistent with this. In addition to developing professional skills, law and medicine both use cases as a way of exposing learners to curricular content. Exposure to cases in law provides a way to learn some of the substantive law within a particular area, and to learn about legal procedures. Many of the uses of cases in medicine address the same goal, while PBL is intended to stimulate self-directed learning and the integration of curricular content.

Motivate Students. These goals for learning outcomes are often accompanied by a more pedagogical goal—to motivate and enhance learning. For example, the chapter on teaching with cases in business indicates that cases engage students by actively involving them in real-world problems. Similarly, learning of abstract scientific principles in medical education can be motivated by cases that show their clinical relevance.

6. Strengths and Limitations of Case Teaching

The wide variety of ways of teaching with cases allows the instructor to draw on their many strengths and to identify and incorporate means of overcoming their limitations. In this chapter, we will focus on some of the issues that have been raised with some regularity; the tips and strategies discussed in the rest of this guide will provide options for case teachers to overcome the limitations.

Strengths of Case Teaching

Active Learning. Case teaching requires students to accept responsibility for their own learning. Students teach themselves in the preparation process, which involves finding meaning in the information they are given; this is an active process rather than a passive learning experience. In class discussions under the guidance of the instructor, students direct the dialogue to areas that stimulate their curiosity. As a result, students can tailor their learning to their individual needs.

Practical Application. Students learn by applying theories to real-world situations and by discovering the limitations of theories as they attempt to apply them. This, in turn, helps them develop new theories. The process is akin to the Kolb (1984) learning cycle, in which students learn by applying a theory, reflecting on the results of the application, developing generalizations, testing their generalizations, and re-applying the revised theory.

Levels of Learning. Case teaching allows students to learn analytical and judgement skills. Benjamin Bloom classified educational goals into knowledge, comprehension, application, analysis, synthesis, and evaluation. Cases emphasize application of theories to real-world events and analysis of information presented. Students are expected to pull the analysis together and draw conclusions (synthesis), as well as to weigh the evidence and make choices (evaluation).

Exposure. Because students analyze a large and varied number of cases over the course of a degree program, they are exposed to a much wider set of situations than they can normally expect in their professional lives. Students learn to compare and contrast the application of theories across a range of different situations. As a result, they can approach new situations with a great wealth of experience and generalized knowledge.

Student Interaction. Cases provide a focal point for the exchange of student experience. Students contribute a wealth of individual observations, experiences, and rules-of-thumb that can be reassessed and shared with others in case discussions.

Engagement. Cases provide students with ambiguous problems that require analysis, careful reflection, and judgement. Students become very involved and interested in the process of finding a solution. For instructors, case teaching can be highly stimulating as no two discussions of the same case are ever the same.

Limitations of Case Teaching

Against the above strengths, however, cases have some limitations.

Communicating Theory. Case teaching has been considered by some to be an inefficient way of communicating theory. In law, in particular, students read several different cases reaching opposite conclusions with similar facts. Students may be so focused on the facts of the cases that they lose their focus on the broad underlying principles.

In other disciplines, the success of cases in communicating theory depends on the students' ability to learn by induction, to generalize from specific circumstances. Students may remember the case, but will they remember the lessons to draw from it?

Approximation of Reality. Cases cannot fully replicate the circumstances faced in practice by doctors, lawyers, managers, teachers, or engineers. The information in written cases is considerably more organized than in the real world. With cases, students are typically not required to listen to clients or patients, investigate facts, clarify goals and interests, negotiate, or plan their approach. They are typically given considerable time to reflect, a luxury not afforded to professionals. As a result, students may become "case experts" without developing real-world professional skills.

Student Maturity. Cases require students to take a degree of responsibility for their own learning. This may be challenging for some undergraduate students, especially those who have not been exposed to cases before. Students must also be comfortable speaking in class and being challenged; moreover, many students do not have any training in listening actively to their peers.

Participation Requirements. Since class participation is often an important component of case learning, many instructors grade students on the level and quality of their participation in discussions. However, the evaluation of participation is controversial as it is often unclear to students what represents a 'good comment' as opposed to a bad one. More assertive students may dominate the discussion and the process may encourage non-productive competition at the expense of supportive learning.

7. Principles for Effective Use of Cases

The following chapters provide a discussion of the major issues that arise in case teaching: case selection and writing, and how to facilitate and evaluate students' learning. We set the stage for a detailed examination of these issues by discussing two fundamental principles that should shape our overall approach to teaching using cases. We then summarize some key principles of effective teaching and learning with cases that are discussed in more detail in later chapters.

Overall Principles

Instructional Alignment. There should be consistency between our goals, the characteristics of the students, and our teaching methods. Specifically, choices about cases must be connected to the preparedness of students, the immediate objectives of the course, and the larger goals of their program. For example, different implementations of cases can work towards or against the program goal of promoting self-directed learning.

Regular Self-Evaluation. Chapter 6 discussed some of the potential limits of teaching with cases. If we are to recognize these when they occur and make changes that are effective, we should evaluate our teaching on a regular basis. It can be useful to ask ourselves and our students questions about the usefulness of the case as a learning tool, the adequacy and helpfulness of resources, the usefulness of activities associated with studying the case, and how well the experience has helped students prepare for subsequent assessments or real-world activities.

Key Principles of Effective Teaching and Learning with Cases

This part of the chapter summarizes some of the key principles of effective teaching and learning with cases. The principles are divided into categories based on their role in designing, planning, implementing, and evaluating a case-based class. These topics are addressed in more detail in the remainder of the guide.

Before the Course Begins

Establish Clear Pedagogical Objectives. Effective case teaching is based on a clear sense of what the course is intended to achieve, and how each case contributes to it. Thus it is important to set learning goals not just for the course as a whole, but also for each individual case. See the discussion in Chapter 10.

Select Appropriate Cases. As instructor, you give up some control when you adopt case teaching. However, you exercise some direction over the learning process through the materials—cases and associated readings—you select. Chapter 8 provides a discussion of the considerations involved in case selection and development; if you intend to write your own cases, read Chapter 9.

Establish the Learning Model. You will need to plan your approach to teaching with cases, determine the balance of lecture versus discussion, and decide how you will conduct the discussion. See Chapter 10.

At the Beginning of the Course

Set Expectations for Students. Students, especially those who are not familiar with case learning, need to hear early on about your expectations for preparation and class participation. It also helps to give students who are new to cases some practice in the process (perhaps through a short case discussion in the first session). See Chapter 12 for a discussion of the importance of setting expectations, preparing for class, and other implementation issues.

Establish a Clear and Fair Grading Model. While the assessment of learning from cases is often subjective, students should understand your criteria and what you expect them to demonstrate. Chapter 11 discusses the issue of assessing learning from cases.

Before Class

Prepare Content and Process. It is just as important to prepare the case discussion process as the case itself. In preparing the case, you should be sufficiently familiar with the facts of the case and how they may be analyzed to address student questions. Preparation of the discussion involves sequencing the discussion in relation to session objectives, and developing a board plan. See the discussion of preparation in Chapter 10.

In Class

Monitor the Discussion Flow. Keep in mind the session objectives as you direct the discussion. If the students go off on tangents, you will need to evaluate quickly whether the detour provides worthwhile learning or whether they should be brought back to your intended flow. See Chapter 10 for a variety of methods of conducting a case discussion.

Provide Effective Feedback. As the discussion proceeds, you will need to listen carefully to student comments and provide appropriate feedback. Some guidelines for providing effective feedback are given in Chapter 11.

After Class

Reflect on the Discussion. Since each case discussion is different, it is helpful to keep a record of the discussion as an input to future sessions. If you are grading participation, you should record each student's participation as soon as possible after class. See Chapter 11.

Part 3: Tips And Strategies For Case Teaching

This last part of the guide provides some concrete suggestions for bringing cases into the classroom. Chapter 8 addresses case selection and development. Chapter 9 provides tips for writing your own cases. How cases can be used to facilitate learning is explored in Chapter 10. Chapter 11 explores how student learning might be evaluated when the case method is employed. Finally, Chapter 12 provides some reflections and concrete suggestions on how to effectively implement the case method in your classroom.

8. Case Selection and Development

Although teaching by case discussion usually means allowing students to participate in their own learning, as instructor you can direct the content, process, and tone of the course through careful selection of the materials to be discussed. For example, you can arrange cases in increasing levels of difficulty to build skills and knowledge progressively, or you can arrange them based on theme or type of analysis required.

Types of Cases

Cases vary greatly in the types of issues they cover, the information they provide, their level of difficulty, their level of notoriety, the media they use, and the range of tasks required of students. Since case learning usually involves decisions in some form, we have classified cases using a model of decision making, shown in Figure 8.1.

Once students understand and analyze the information presented, they may be required to define the problem, conduct further analysis, make a decision, or develop policies to guide future decisions. The information provided in different types of cases leads them to different stages in the decision process, with either a known or an unknown outcome. The dotted lines in Figure 8.1 indicate that the ultimate outcome of the case may either be given within the case itself, or you may later reveal it to the students.

A description of each of the major case types is given below along with comments on the educational goals to which each is most suited.

Application Cases. Application cases are designed to give students practice at using analytical frameworks or tools. As an example, accounting students may be presented with a balance sheet and asked to compute financial ratios for the company. Such cases may be simple or complex, but their focus tends to be narrower than other types of case. As a result, data tend to be clustered so as to highlight cause-effect relationships and lead students to

Fig. 8.1   Types of Case According to Decision Requirements

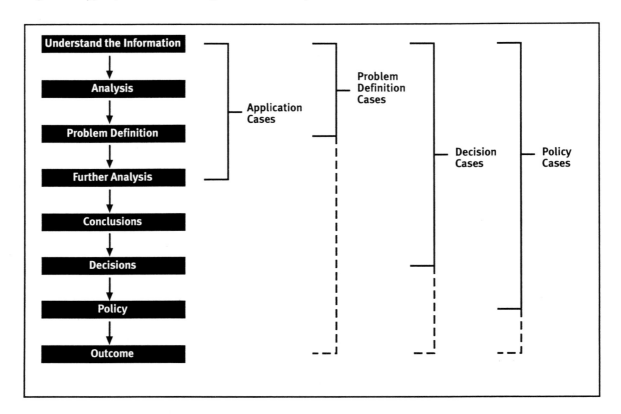

application of the concept or tool. This may not always be purely an application exercise, however: students may be required to understand theory and to exercise judgement in selecting the appropriate tool and in interpreting the results.

Appropriate Goals: Application cases primarily help students develop new concepts or understand analytical techniques.

Problem-Definition Cases. Problem-definition cases require students to identify what may be an ambiguous problem underlying the information presented. In medical cases, for example, diverse symptoms presented by a patient may have one underlying cause, or in a business case, what initially appears to be an ethical problem of how to lay off employees may be a trade off between the welfare of some employees relative to others. The problem is not immediately apparent, and there may not be a "right answer." There also may be more than one problem. Students need to absorb the information in the case, analyze and reflect on it, and weigh the evidence to develop a point of view.

With problem-definition cases, the outcome can often reveal the nature and dimensions of the problem, so such cases do not usually include information about the outcome. However, students often want to know the outcome, and it can be instructive to reveal it during the class discussion or in a subsequent class.

Appropriate Goals: Problem-definition cases help students acquire skills in analyzing real-world problems and in observing patterns in the information presented.

Decision Cases. Decision cases usually provide students with (sometimes extensive) background on a particular problem in the expectation that they will come to a decision—such as the appropriate medical treatment, an effective administrative approach, or an exemplary in-flight manoeuvre—based on the information provided. The information presented may be qualitative, quantitative, or both. Students are required to apply skills in analysis, synthesis, and evaluation as well as their knowledge of the theory.

The case may or may not include information about the actual outcome: what decision was made and its results. Withholding information about the outcome introduces an element of drama by allowing students to put themselves in the decision-maker's shoes, while revealing the outcome in the case allows students to 'dissect' the decision with the benefit of hindsight. With the growth of the World-Wide Web, it can be difficult to conceal the outcome from motivated students.

Appropriate Goals: Decision cases help students draw conclusions from their analysis, evaluate their results, and consider the consequences of their decisions.

Policy Cases. Policy cases allow students to consider the broader implications of a decision. Students are expected to think beyond the immediate decision to its future impact, and to develop strategies for future decisions in similar situations: a settlement with an autoworkers' union becomes the bargaining 'floor' for the next contract negotiations in a different setting; or the particular facts of one patient's psychiatric disorder results in the development of prescribing guidelines for the psychiatric disorder generally.

As with decision cases, the outcome of policy cases may or may not be known to the students. However, revealing the outcome of a policy case can have its advantages: where the outcome is known, as is typically the case in law, students can focus more closely on its broader implications rather than on the details of the decision itself.

Appropriate Goals: Policy cases help students evaluate decisions in broader terms and develop mature judgement.

In some courses, the objectives will be primarily about understanding concepts and the instructor will use mostly analytical cases, perhaps introducing problem-definition cases at the end of the course. In other courses, advanced students may already have a good understanding of the theoretical concepts and need to develop skills in evaluation and judgement; here the emphasis will be on decision cases and perhaps policy cases.

Selecting Cases

While the above categories provide some guidance to the types of cases available and the educational outcomes associated with each, the selection of cases and their sequencing in a course can involve a wide range of issues beyond the nature of the case. Table 8.1 gives a list of factors to consider in selecting cases for a course; in developing this table, we have taken account of those factors used in case selection by STLHE members (see Chapter 4) along with other criteria found in the literature.

Course Factors. Course factors include the objectives of the course and of the specific session. As noted earlier, different learning objectives imply the use of different types of cases. Beyond the type of learning you want to achieve, the case should match your 'content' objectives for the session. Some cases, however, can be used for multiple purposes and you may lead students in the direction you wish. In marketing education courses, cases on advertising often include data on customer segments, customer behaviour, and competitive activities, depending on the information the instructor chooses to emphasize.

In addition to objectives, consider the case's timing within the course. Do the students have the skills to analyze the case? To what other cases have they been exposed and how do those cases connect with this one? (It is also important to check with your colleagues within the department to see whether they have already used the cases you are considering.)

Case Factors. Case factors include difficulty, length, richness, and realism. There are at least three ways in which cases can become more **difficult**[5]:

- The amount of data in the case and the way it is organized can increase difficulty. Is it clustered to lead the reader to certain types of analysis? For example, a patient may present a diverse array of symptoms, only a few of which are relevant.
- The case may or may not give clear signals to students as to the type of analysis required. The statement "a comprehensive market analysis was required" essentially leaves it up to the students to decide the nature and scope of the analysis.
- The value system underlying a case, which refers to the set of criteria that students will use to analyze the case, may vary in difficulty. In less difficult cases, this will be spelt out more or less clearly; in more difficult cases, students will be expected to develop their own values. Students may be left to decide, for example, on the societal impact of a Supreme Court decision, with little guidance given on what aspects of social welfare should be considered.

The appropriate level of difficulty for a given course depends on the course objectives, the nature of the material, the students' level of knowledge and experience with cases, and their

---

[5] Some readers may be familiar with Maufette-Leenders, Erskine, and Leenders' "Case Difficulty Cube," whose difficulty dimensions—Presentation, Analytical, and Conceptual—approximate those given here.

facility with each of the difficulty dimensions. In general, it makes sense to increase the level of difficulty on each of these three dimensions as the course proceeds. However, as new concepts are introduced during the course, it may be appropriate to return to simpler cases from time to time to ensure that the students understand the concepts before moving on to more complex ones.

A related factor is the **length** of the case. Clearly, this relates to how much time it is reasonable to expect the students to spend reading and preparing the case. If you plan to hand out the case in class, it should be short enough to read within a few minutes yet rich enough to provoke an in-depth discussion. If you are assigning other readings along with the case, consider the students' total workload for the session.

The degree of **richness** of a case refers to its potential for a stimulating discussion. The case should lend itself to more than one interpretation, and be sufficiently complex that a variety of facts can be brought to bear. There should be more than one right answer and much of the class will be spent discussing the tradeoffs involved in adopting each of several potential solutions.

Finally, the degree of **realism** of a case can be an important factor. The intent of case teaching is to simulate real-world problems, and cases should therefore represent problems students are likely to encounter in their professional lives.

Student Factors. Student factors include the characteristics of the students themselves and the 'student appeal' of the case. Student characteristics include their level of theoretical knowledge and skill, as well as their experience with cases. However, lack of theoretical knowledge or case experience need not be a barrier to introducing cases. Some instructors prefer to alternate cases with lectures to develop students' theoretical base as the course proceeds, while others use cases from the word 'go' and interject with carefully timed mini-lectures to build students' knowledge as required.

The appeal of a given case to students can be an important factor in their level of motivation to prepare and discuss it. The following are some of the attributes of cases that appeal most to students:

- well written: clear, lively
- interesting characters
- interesting story
- action, drama, and realism
- relevant to the reader's interests
- clear focus and substantive purpose
- allow the reader to empathize with the central character

An additional quality that may appeal to students is fame or infamy. Working on a famous case, such as that of Phineas Gage in neuropsychology, or *R. v. Morgentaler* (the case that decriminalized abortion in Canada) in law, can give students a sense that their discussion is important beyond the confines of the classroom.

Instructor Factors. Instructor factors will also influence your choice of a case. Your own strengths, interests, and competences as a researcher and teacher are important: if you are not 'turned on' by a case, it can be difficult to generate enthusiasm among students. On the other hand, if the issues in a case inspire you, your excitement can be infectious.

The following factors appeal to instructors in choosing cases:

- intellectually and substantively high quality (be careful, instructors are more likely than students to be attracted to cases involving extensive, challenging analysis)
- accompanied by a useful teaching note
- suitable for the amount of time available for the discussion, and for the physical arrangements
- potentially interesting to students

Finally, sharing **responsibility for learning** between you and your students plays an important part in case selection. A case may be little more than a worked-out example of a problem, so that students have relatively little involvement in analyzing it; here, you as the instructor take the primary role and assume a significant share of the responsibility for students' learning. Alternatively, a case may require extensive analysis and value judgement from students, in which case the students will assume primary responsibility for their learning. The class session typically guides students through a comparison of their analyses and perspectives.

9. Case Writing

There are several reasons to write your own case rather than to select one from existing sources. A suitable case may not be available: since there are many criteria for selecting cases, it can be difficult to find a case that not only meets your objectives for the course and the session, but also challenges students at an appropriate level, provides a compelling story for your class, and can realistically be prepared and discussed in the time available.

An additional reason for developing a case is that you may be fortunate enough to encounter a situation that will make an engaging story for students or that makes an important point related to your course. A practising physician, for example, may come across a patient with a puzzling set of symptoms, or an educator may encounter a difficult ethical problem with a student that would make an interesting case.

A third reason for developing your own cases is that the process of development makes you intimately familiar with the situation and 'living' the analysis of the case allows you to think of the directions students are likely to take with the case. There is a downside to this, though: you may become so close to the case that its subtleties seem obvious to you where they are obscure to students, and it becomes tempting to 'take over' the analysis for them.

Cases can provide fodder for research based on real-world situations. Teaching cases often pose problems that have not been solved by researchers and may indicate boundary conditions for existing theories. Research cases are regularly published in the medical literature for similar reasons.

For the purposes of this guide, we will concentrate here on writing a teaching case: because research cases are not written for a student audience, they follow a different process that is tangential to our purposes here. We also concentrate on written cases, as opposed to video or interactive cases, since most cases are still presented in this form and because the disciplines underlying written cases also apply to other forms with appropriate refinements for the medium.

Ten Characteristics of a Good Case

As shown in Table 9.1, a good case not only provides the information to solve a problem, but also demands that students use critical thinking. Beyond these qualities, a case should have the quality of a good 'story': the issues discussed should be engaging to students, and the case should be written in a way that commands their attention:

Underlying these ten characteristics are three broader themes: your case should be based on a theory, pose a controversial problem that the students can analyze, and be interesting to read.

Table 9.1 Ten Characteristics of a Good Case

1.	Has pedagogic utility
2.	Represents a general issue beyond the case itself
3.	Tells an engaging story
4.	Focuses on an interest-arousing, controversial issue
5.	Poses a problem that has no obvious right answer
6.	Creates empathy with the central characters
7.	Requires the reader to use the information in the case to address the problem
8.	Requires the reader to think critically and analytically to address the problem
9.	Brevity—has just enough information for a good analysis
10.	Is relevant to students

The Case Writing Process

Writing a case is both an analytical and a creative exercise. The analytical side should be tailored to your own field and to the particular issues you are interested in teaching through the case. However, as renowned Harvard case teacher Malcolm P. McNair wrote, "case writing is an art, and a good case is a definite literary accomplishment" (1954). The creative exercise involves building a story—a drama—that will engage students and motivate them to delve deeply into the issues. As a drama, it should have principal and supporting actors, an opening act that draws the reader in, an inciting incident, and a concluding dilemma that the student is left to resolve. As you plan and execute your case research, be sure to gather information that will help with both aspects of case writing.

An outline of the basic process is given in Table 9.2. Depending on your field and on the nature of the case you are writing, you may want to place more or less emphasis on different parts of this process.

Table 9.2   The Case Writing Process

Preliminary Research/Initial Contact

Planning Phase
- Case Prospectus
- Research Plan
- Timetable

Research
- Library research
- Field research

Drafting
- Case draft
- Critical review

Editing/Revising

Trial class

Final Version

Teaching Note

Release and Publication

The process usually begins with some form of **preliminary research**, for a case based on library research, or an **initial contact** with a practitioner in the relevant field. In either instance, it is helpful to begin with a reasonably clear idea of what you are looking for: the key ideas you want to get across, and where the case fits in your course. Library research can provide accounts of dilemmas or decisions faced by practitioners in your field that may make interesting cases for students. Alternatively, organizations or individuals may be willing to contribute information to the development of a case. They have a variety of motivations for doing this: the contact with academics and students may keep them abreast of research in their field, they may anticipate that the development of a case will help them solve similar problems in the future, or they may just want to make a contribution to the education process.

The **planning phase** is critically important to developing a useful case. It is good practice to develop a written case prospectus that outlines the purpose of the case and provides a rough framework. A case prospectus can consist of the following sections:

- The subject, or the basic subject matter of the case—for example, sexual harassment in the workplace—should be stated.
- The intended audience for the case should be detailed—the level and age of the students (first year undergraduate, advanced undergraduate, graduate, etc.). Also consider the prerequisite level of theoretical knowledge to understand and analyze the case: this will provide guidance on how complex your case should be.
- The teaching objectives, including where the case fits in the course, the theory you intend to teach with it, and the level of learning you expect should be set out. There may be theoretical readings that will ultimately accompany the case, and it is also helpful to identify these early on.
- An outline of the narrative structure of the case should be provided. How did the situation arise? What was the inciting incident? What were its implications? What are the students (implicitly or explicitly) being asked to do at the end of the case? A framework for a basic case outline is given in Table 9.3.

Table 9.3   A Basic Case Outline

Introduction/Summary

Key actors

Opening/beginning of story

Key incident or episode

Additional events/implications

Climax of story/moment of decision

Closing

Appendices

Once you have outlined the basic purpose and content of the case, a research plan will help guide your efforts. Since the issue here is what information is required for students to complete the case analysis, this exercise calls for a clear sense of the teaching objectives of the case and the analysis that will be demanded. List the key pieces of information needed and your research strategies for obtaining them: library research, field research, interviews (Who? What questions?). Develop a timetable for these activities and a set of milestones to get you to your draft case. These can be summarized in a research plan, as shown in Table 9.4:

Table 9.4   Research Plan for (Case)

Teaching Objectives:

1. _____

2. _____

3. _____

Analysis	Information Required	Field	Library Research	Completion Date

Case **research** consists of both library research and field research. Library research is usually needed to develop some background knowledge of the issue or the case situation before embarking on interviews. Some cases are composed entirely of library research. A great deal of case work, however, relies on field work in the form of visits to, and interviews with, key players. In conducting case interviews, it is important to keep in mind that the goal of the process is to develop a case that will not only have some substantive content but a story that will engage student interest. For this reason, a case interview is not just about 'getting the facts' but is a creative exercise in identifying characters and points of dramatic tension.

In **drafting** the case, keep in mind the characteristics of a good case given above. This means paying attention not just to the facts, but also to how good a 'read' your case is. Resist the temptation to put everything in: you are interested in providing students with enough information to solve the problem, but not in overwhelming them. Strive for absolute clarity throughout; define terms as appropriate. Avoid unnecessary jargon and technical terminology unless you are sure the students will be familiar with it. Use quotations, anecdotes, and description to make the characters come alive.

There are two schools of thought on the appropriate length of a case: those who believe that a case should provide just enough information to solve the problem and have a rich discussion, and those who believe that inclusion of irrelevant information forces students to sort through it and decide what is critical. Shorter cases particularly should be based on a compelling issue and the data provided open to several interpretations in order for the discussion to be sufficiently rich. With longer cases, students may need more guidance with the analysis and may also need to be convinced that the extra effort is worthwhile.

Once the case has been drafted, critical review will help you refine it. To make sure you have the facts straight, seek comments from the organization, individual, or group that is the subject of the case. For comments on pedagogy and on how well the case represents the theoretical issues, seek the input of a colleague. For comments on the story, interest level, and possible logical gaps, seek the comments of a student.

Once you have **edited and revised** the case, it is not complete until you have "road tested" it by conducting several **trial classes**; since the discussion will be different each time you teach it, the more experience you can get with it, the better. It is also helpful to ask the students for feedback on the case itself when they have been through the experience of preparing and discussing it. When you have developed a good sense of the issues students bring up in discussion and any sticking points such as gaps in information provided, prepare your **final version**.

Table 9.5: Outline of a Standard Teaching Note

Abstract
- Brief summary of the scenario and the issues involved

Teaching Objectives
- Appropriate learning goals

Prerequisites
- Appropriate student group or level
- Suggested courses or situations in which the case may be used

Assignment Questions
Analysis
- Based on assignment questions

Postscript
- Any information on the ultimate outcome of the case

Class Plan
- Suggestions for how to run the class – what issues to introduce in what order, etc.

Board Plan
- Suggestions on how to record the discussion on the board

Your experience in preparing the case and in teaching it is invaluable to others who may want to use it: as noted in Chapter 8, faculty place a high value on having a good-quality **teaching note** accompanying the case. A teaching note suggests assignment questions for students, provides an analysis, and gives some approaches to teaching the case, such as which issues can be introduced in what order, how the board may be organized, etc. A standard outline of a teaching note is given in Table 9.5.

Prior to **publication**, the subject of the case should sign a **release**: this can be an important issue as organizations or individuals may baulk at publication of confidential information. For this reason, it is important to make it clear from the outset that your ultimate intent is to publish the case, and to disguise information or identities if necessary to make it easier for your subject to commit to public release.

10. Using Cases to Facilitate Learning

The advantages of the case method have been outlined in some detail in the preceding chapters. They include that the learning is student centred, that students are exposed to the real world, develop a broad range of skills, embrace a professional perspective, learn to think independently, and become engaged in the material. Given those advantages of the case method, this part of the guide discusses the different learning formats in which the case method may be taught. The first section addresses the teaching styles that an instructor might adopt. The next section provides some tips on how to structure a case method class.

Method of Instruction

Your choice of method of instruction should flow at least in part from the educational objectives articulated for the course. Some of the general objectives of a case method class are outlined in Chapter 5. For example, if an instructor's objective is simply to impart knowledge about the case, there may be some circumstances under which a lecture style is appropriate. On the other hand, if an objective is to provide a setting where students develop their oral argument skills, it may make sense for you to require or encourage student participation.

In addition to the course objectives, the size of the class may dictate the method of instruction. Large classes (for example, over 100 students) may be conducive to the Socratic method or to a lecture style, but it may be difficult to conduct a satisfactory discussion. What constitutes a 'large class' will vary based on your own skills and patience. Some instructors may be able to facilitate a discussion with 100 people, and some may find a discussion-based approach impossible when the class has more than 20 students. It would be a particularly unusual instructor who had enough skill to effectively conduct an entirely discussion-based class with more than 100 students.

This part of the chapter classifies case teaching styles into three broad teaching approaches. Of course, these distinctions are artificial, and many instructors use some hybrid version. In addition, most instructors use some combination of these different approaches depending on the objectives of a particular class, or even a topic within a class.

Socratic Method. The Socratic method has been intricately linked with the case method approach to learning. In its strictest application, an instructor in a Socratic classroom asks questions about the case under review, never providing the class with the 'right' answer and providing guidance only through the questioning process. Usually, student participation is mandatory. Students are called on and required to answer the instructor's questions.

The Socratic method has significant benefits:

- Everyone has to participate, and so everyone develops a stake in the learning.
- Students may develop skills for self-evaluation. Students hear the comments made by others in the class, and can witness the instructor's response. They are able to test themselves to see which questions they were able to answer and which they were not.
- The classroom can seem exciting. The uncertainty of being called on can be invigorating for some students.
- Students feel responsible for the material covered. If students are not prepared to participate, other people in the class will notice. Therefore, students may work together to prepare prior to class.
- It can be used in classrooms of any size. No matter how many students are in a class, an instructor can always call names from a class list, or simply direct questions to individuals in the 'audience.'
- Students feel challenged and stimulated. The Socratic method puts students on the spot.
- Students can receive immediate feedback on their analysis. Instructors are able to tell students immediately whether their responses made sense, were consistent, were thorough, and so on. The rest of the class may also benefit.

Critics have also identified some disadvantages:

- Students may feel that they are closely (and sometimes unfairly) scrutinized. Some students may be chosen more than others to answer questions, or feel they are chosen on days when they appear to be particularly unprepared. This can lead to feelings of anger and resentment.
- Students may feel anxious. Even when students are prepared, some of them feel anxious about having to think fast. The enormous fear of embarrassment experienced by some students can lead them to dread their Socratic classes.

- It does not help students develop cooperative skills. Although not an inevitable result, the Socratic method sometimes leads students to develop a competitive attitude to preparation for class. Also, given that the general method is to call on one particular individual in class, students can feel very isolated when called upon to respond.
- It may be inefficient or the pace of the class may seem slow. It can take a long time to work through all of the important aspects of a case when the instructor asks one question at a time. Students may be slow to respond, or it may take a number of questions to elicit a rather simple point. Students who have become skilled at the case method often feel frustrated by the pace of the classes.
- It reinforces the position of instructor as the authority in the classroom. Because the instructor does the questioning, it is clear that the instructor is in control of the class.
- It may be experienced by students differently based on their backgrounds. Some students may find direct questioning, which can at times be confrontational, unsettling or upsetting.

The Socratic method can be useful in many classroom settings. It ensures class participation, it requires that students prepare in advance because they know they may be called upon, it can be employed regardless of the size of the class, it allows the instructor to provide immediate feedback, and it allows the instructor to exercise at least some control over the direction of the class discussion.

The approach may be inappropriate, however, if the instructor wants to foster cooperation among students, has students who are insecure about the subject matter, or when the instructor would like the students to be more responsible for the direction of the classes.

Class Discussion. There are two differences between the Socratic approach and a class discussion approach. First, in a class discussion, the instructor's role may vary, but the instructor is not necessarily the ultimate conductor. In leading an examination of cases using a class discussion, the instructor may, for example, provide answers to students' questions, or may decide not to say anything at all. The instructor in this case can usefully focus the discussion and move the students to new issues when the discussion seems to have run its course. Students may work together as a larger class or be broken into small teams to discuss particular cases.

Second, the class exercises more direction over the discussion. Although the instructor has normally chosen the material for study, the students in the class are more actively involved in directing the learning. (The degree to which this section is only a general statement of approach cannot be overemphasized. For example, some instructors do not even choose the material for study, leaving that decision to the students as well.)

A class discussion-based model has a number of advantages:

- Students direct the learning. The students can lead the course in the directions they find interesting.
- Students identify the issues and analyze the case largely independently. The instructor can act more as an assistant or guide than as a conductor of the discussion.
- The instructor can use a range of possible learning formats: small groups, writing exercises, think-pair-share, and so on. There is lots of room to vary the routine.
- The instructor can take a more or less active role depending on the class needs. The instructor can, for example, provide clear directions on analyzing the first case in a particular area of study, but then in the next class simply let students work through a similar case on their own.
- It leaves scope to develop cooperative skills. Students can be required to work in different groups and develop team-building skills in addition to acquiring the substantive information about the case.
- Students feel challenged and motivated. Because students are directing the learning, they feel personally involved in the material being discussed.
- Students can receive immediate feedback on their analysis. The instructor has many opportunities in facilitating discussions to provide feedback, where appropriate. This feedback can be individual (and delivered individually), or can be delivered to the class as a whole.

There are also disadvantages to implementing a class discussion-based model:

- Discussion can be hard to implement in large classes. The teacher could, however, break the class into groups to conduct discussions among themselves. On a very basic level, with students working in groups, classrooms can get very noisy and it can be difficult to hear. Where classes are quite large it can be difficult for an instructor to have any real sense of what many of the groups are doing.
- The class can become unruly or undirected. If students feel too removed from the instructor they can stray from assigned task into discussion of social events. This can result in students feeling like the class is a waste of time or that they are not learning as much as they had hoped.
- Students may be oppositional or argumentative with one another. If some students are particularly aggressive or difficult, their participation can make others feel uncomfortable. This is most likely to become a problem where topics are sensitive.
- It may be difficult to facilitate student participation. If an instructor does not rely on an involuntary method of participation sometimes student willingness to participate flags or students simply are not prepared.

The discussion approach to the case method generally works very well. Students are actively involved in the learning process, cooperation can be fostered, and instructors develop a good sense of what the students have learned by listening to their conversations. There are drawbacks, however, where the class size is particularly large, or where students are unprepared.

Lecture Method. Although we have some reservations about presenting lectures as a method of conducting a case class, given the predominance of lecture-style classes in some disciplines, we thought we would address it in this part of the guide. Many of the benefits of case teaching are lost when the lecture method is employed. Using a lecture format, the instructor walks students through each of the cases—revealing for students the relevant issues, dilemmas, counter-arguments, and possible resolutions. Students are expected to learn how to reason through cases themselves by watching their (skilled) instructor engage in that process.

Advantages of the lecture method:

- A great deal of substantive material can be covered in relatively little time. Because the instructor simply walks through the material, time is not spent on material that is irrelevant and the discussion never needs to stray from the focus of the case.
- It can be implemented in very large classes more easily than other methods. No matter how many students are in a class, as long as students can hear, a lecture format can be employed.
- The instructor can model how to analyze a case. Instructors are presumably skilled at analyzing a case. While watching someone do something is not as good as doing it one's self, there is some benefit to students witnessing a skilled instructor describe how he or she would think through a case.

Disadvantages of the lecture method:

- Students do not necessarily learn how to reason through a case on their own. If students do not prepare in advance, they may simply rely on the instructor to provide them with the 'answers' in class. Students may memorize the answers, but never understand the process of getting to them.
- It does not teach any oral skills. Because students rarely talk when lectures are used (except to ask the occasional question) they are not confronted with the necessity of articulating their thoughts aloud.
- Students may not feel challenged. Students can often walk away from a lecture without having felt engaged in the material.

As noted above, the lecture format is not an ideal way to conduct a case method class. It does not bring students into the learning, it does not foster cooperation, students learn few skills, and it can be extremely dull. On the other hand, where a substantial amount of material must be conveyed quickly, or where class sizes are simply too large for regular discussions, the lecture method may be used. In these circumstances, it might make sense to try to incorporate at least some discussions into the class to derive a number of the benefits from the previously discussed methods.

Conducting a Case Method Class

Preparing for and facilitating a case method class can be quite different from preparing for a lecture course based on a textbook. This section of the chapter provides some suggestions for preparing for class, running the classroom discussion, and process after class.

Preparing for Class. In preparing for class, you should be attentive to both the content and process of the session. In designing a particular class the most important thing to keep in mind are your objectives for the session and the course as a whole. Both the content and process of the class should clearly reflect those objectives.

Here are some suggestions for preparing for class:

- Consider the sequence of classes generally, ensuring that the material flows logically. The structure of a course as a whole is important, and should make some sense to you. Why does one topic follow another? What are the building blocks for the content?
- Develop objectives for the class. Each class should have a specific objective or set of objectives. One of the greatest dangers is trying to do too much in one class. Set only a small number of objectives, but make sure to achieve them.
- Consider the amount of time that should be spent on each case (if there is more than one case in a session). The timing of the class is important. Again, don't try to be overly ambitious. Make sure to leave time for questions and discussion.
- Review materials and notes for completeness, organization, and logic. There is nothing worse than getting into a class and discovering that you have left half of your material at home or that you forgot to finish a point in your notes.
- Prepare questions for discussion. Think about what key points you want students to derive from the case and focus on developing questions that draw out those points. Develop some simple questions and some more complicated ones. It is often best to begin with some straightforward questions and then move to questions that are more complex.
- Check the classroom arrangements. Make sure that students will be able to hear you no matter where they are sitting. See if you will be able to walk up and down the aisles in the classroom. If you plan on using some kind of teaching tool

(blackboards, videos, computers, and so on), make sure those tools are available in the room. Ensure that everyone can see or hear your teaching tools.

- Confirm that the technology works. Even if everything is available in your classroom, it may not all be working. Check to make sure that overheads turn on, that VCRs are connected to TVs, and so on.

Conducting the Class. It is helpful to plan the beginning, middle, and end of each class, so that students understand where they are in the discussion process. At the beginning of the class it is often helpful to provide a road map. You can capture student interest at the start of the class with something exciting or something requiring their attention. It might be possible, for example, to open with a relevant news story, an interesting question from the materials for the day, or a succinct review of what was covered in the last session.

How you conduct the middle of the class will, of course, depend on your teaching method. In Socratic sessions, you would use the middle of the class to guide the students through the important and interesting aspects of the case using questions. Similarly, in a discussion-based class, you would raise some of the interesting issues to spark discussion and debate among members of the class.

The end of a class is important. Too often classes end with students slamming their books and packing up to leave while the instructor screams a few last points over the noise. End on time. End with something interesting—a question for reflection the next day, identification (by a student) of the most interesting thing that was said in the class discussion, or a summary of the material covered, for example.

After Class. The case method, particularly when you use a discussion-based approach, can bring surprises. Students may ask unexpected questions, raise unexpected discussion points, or get unexpectedly upset about aspects of the case or class discussion. Some cases may seem interesting to you, but spark little discussion. Other cases may seem straightforward, but result in an intense debate. It is useful after class to make some notes on how the cases in that class were received and discussed for future reference. When you pick up your notes in the future you will be grateful for these reminders.

It is also useful to seek feedback from students on the class. Particularly for students unfamiliar with the case method, its adoption can be difficult and disorienting. Feedback can be solicited using a variety of informal and formal mechanisms. For example, you might simply ask a few students lingering after class how things are going—what made sense and did not make sense in that particular class, what they think they are learning both in terms of content and skills. Some instructors designate a 'feedback panel' that they meet periodically to get input on, for example, where the class was moving too quickly, what could be cut, what frustrations the students might have, and so on. A formal survey is also an option. It is also useful to administer your own survey about halfway through the term so that students can give you feedback in time for you to adjust your approach. This input can be extremely helpful in making your teaching more effective.

11. Evaluating Learning from Cases

Case teaching can be a very powerful way of encouraging students to think inductively, or to develop generalizations from particular instances. Students who are exposed to a range of cases over the course of a term or a year have the opportunity to see recurring themes across a diverse range of situations, to draw from these some broad principles, and to appreciate the limitations of theories.

Evaluating learning from cases therefore involves assessing what students understand not just about the theories themselves, but how they apply in practice. Grant Wiggins (1998) provides three elements of educative assessment in general:

- Evaluation should be authentic. Evaluation is authentic when it is based on issues that arise in practice in the real world, as opposed to series of questions divorced from practical context.
- Feedback is critical. Evaluation should improve performance, not just audit it; hence ongoing feedback that leads to improvement is an essential component of evaluation.
- Assessment should promote students' understanding. Authentic evaluation and useful feedback should be the basis for developing understanding, as opposed to rote or superficial knowledge.

In the sections that follow, we elaborate on each of Wiggins' elements, and consider how they apply to some of the more common methods of evaluation in case courses. We conclude with guidelines for effective student assessment in case courses based on the learning from these principles.

Authenticity

Authentic evaluation is all about application: the goal is to learn whether students can apply what they have learned, and whether they can innovate in new situations. An evaluation task is authentic if it:

- is realistic, i.e., replicates real-world situations
- requires judgement and innovation on the part of the student to solve unstructured problems
- asks the student to "do" the subject, instead of reciting, restating, or replicating what he or she has learned
- replicates or simulates the context in which professionals conduct tasks in real life so that students experience the context of the workplace, albeit vicariously

- assesses the student's ability to use a repertoire of knowledge to negotiate a complex task, i.e., is more than just a drill testing a single item of knowledge
- allows appropriate opportunities to rehearse, practise, consult resources, and obtain feedback

In summary, authentic evaluation tests students' ability to apply their knowledge to real-world problems in a context that as closely as possible replicates what they will face in their chosen profession in the future. Since cases require students to learn by applying, the idea of authentic testing is particularly relevant.

Feedback

Feedback is information about how the student did in relation to his or her goals. The best feedback is highly specific, descriptive of actual results, clear to the student, and offered in terms of specific targets and standards. At issue is not whether the student did "well" or "badly," but the extent to which her performance achieved the goals she set out to achieve. Good feedback is like road signs for a motorist—it offers continuous feedback on where the student is relative to where she wants to go.

Effective feedback:

- provides evidence of effect relative to intent
- compares current performance and trend to a successful result or standard, e.g., correct diagnosis in medicine
- is timely, e.g., is immediate where possible and sufficiently timely to be useful
- is frequent and ongoing
- is dominated by descriptive, rather than evaluative, language, e.g., "you did not consider the patient's previous condition in your diagnosis," as opposed to "you did badly in the test"
- is such that the student perceives a specific, tangible effect, later confirmed by a score or grade based on specific criteria
- is related to a result derived from true models or exemplars, i.e., an authentic result, as discussed in the previous section
- enables students to improve through self-assessment and self-adjustment

The process of case discussion can be considered an opportunity to provide students with continuous feedback about their performance as the course proceeds. In a case discussion, feedback comes from other students as well as the instructor as students compare themselves against others; the instructor is, of course, responsible for ensuring that this feedback is constructive and useful.

Understanding

Understanding and knowledge are not the same thing. A student may be able to answer questions on a test, but may not grasp the true significance of an idea or its connections with other important ideas. If we truly understand an idea, we should also be able to adapt it to novel situations because we understand what underlying factors make it work.

Five facets of understanding are relevant to student evaluation:

- Students should be able to provide *sophisticated explanations and interpretations*. Understanding requires clarity and insight about how things work, what they mean, where they connect, and why they matter.
- Deep understanding is suggested by *contextual performance, know-how, and sensitivity*. Students should be able to apply, adapt, and customize knowledge.
- The development of *perspective* is an indication of understanding. Students should be able to see things from multiple vantage points, including what is tacit or assumed.
- The ability to get inside the other person's feelings because of a sense of *empathy*, which includes the capacity to experience the world as the other person experiences it, is a sign of understanding.
- The ability to *know our own intellectual prejudices* and to see how they influence and even determine what we understand is an indication of a high degree of understanding.

Case teaching strives to bring students to a rich level of understanding of the theoretical concepts that underlie the practical scenarios they encounter. In addition to applying the theories, students should be able to identify them and their underlying assumptions through discussion with others who hold differing perspectives. An evaluation scheme for case courses must test for these deeper levels of understanding.

Evaluating Evaluation Methods

In Table 11.1, we evaluate the positive and negative aspects of each of three commonly-used evaluation methods in case courses—participation, case exams, and case assignments—against the principles of authenticity, feedback, and understanding. A discussion of each is provided below.

Table 11.1   Comparing Evaluation Methods in Case Courses

	+/-	Authenticity	Feedback	Understanding
Case Exam	+	• Simulates realistic context • Complex task using a repertoire of skills	• Performance compared against exemplars • Clear evaluation criteria	• Student applies knowledge in unpredicted situation • Can test for ability to appreciate different perspectives
	-	• Artificial setting and time limit may compromise realism	• Instructor feedback only • Delayed feedback	• Time limit can compromise ability to demonstrate sophistication
Class Participation	+	• Simulates realistic context • Complex task using a repertoire of skills • Opportunities for practice	• Feedback from peers and instructor • Ongoing • Timely • Peers can provide positive exemplars	• Demonstrates ability to appreciate different perspectives • Student develops self-knowledge through feedback • Multiple cases develop diverse understanding
	-	• Group pressure may discourage students from revealing personal 'real' criteria or issues	• Difficulty in remembering everyone's contribution • Difficulty in setting criteria and weightings • Negative peer comments can discourage shy students	• Time limitations may conceal sophistication of understanding • Shy students may not readily reveal their understanding
Written case assignment	+	• Simulates realistic context • Complex task using a repertoire of skills • Provides time to develop rich analysis	• Performance compared against exemplars • Clear evaluation criteria • Enables students to improve in later assignments	• Student can demonstrate sophistication • Multiple assignments develop contextual knowledge
	-	• Extended time may not be realistic	• Instructor feedback only • Delayed feedback	• Limited perspective in individual assignments

Case Exam

A case exam is one in which students are presented with a case and asked to provide a report in written or oral form. The exam is usually time-limited, and students may or may not receive the case in advance. Open-book exams of this type are common.

In terms of our three principles, case exams do provide a degree of realism (authentricity), which to some extent is compromised by the time limit (some will argue, however, that time constraints are a feature of professional life). Feedback can (or rather should, as much as possible) be based on clear criteria, but–especially with written assignments is–often delayed by the grading process. Usually, feedback in such an exam comes only from the instructor so the student has little opportunity to compare his or her performance with that of peers.

Case exams can test for understanding, especially in the dimension of sophistication. Students are required to apply their knowledge in a new situation, and this demands that they understand the underlying elements of the theory, how they connect, and why they are important. While the case exam can test for sophistication, time constraints may make it difficult for students to demonstrate it.

In summary, case exams can provide rich information about how well students understand and can apply the theory in a somewhat realistic context. They are potentially compromised, however, by time constraints.

Class Participation

Participation in class discussions is commonly tracked and graded in case courses. In some schools, class participation can account for up to 50% of a student's final grade for the course. This places intense pressure on instructors to provide clear criteria for quality participation and to keep careful records of who is contributing in each class and what they said. Some instructors resort to having a teaching assistant attend the class and keep a record; inevitably, participation at this level is a 'hothouse' environment in which students compete intensely for airtime.

There are good reasons for the popularity of participation as an evaluation tool. Like case exams, it provides a simulation of the real world—perhaps a more realistic one because of the absence of a rigid time constraint. Because it is continuous, it provides students with opportunities to practise and improve. For some students, however, class participation is highly intimidating and may be more a test of courage in speaking in front of groups than of understanding of the subject matter.

Participation provides the opportunity for continuous, timely feedback. Moreover, because students learn by observing each other and listening to each others' comments on their work, a great deal of feedback can come from peers rather than the instructor as a figure of authority. The flip side of this is that peers may not be skilled in providing non-evaluative feedback. The difficulties involved in tracking student contributions also can contribute to a perception that participation assessment is unfair.

On the dimension of understanding, participation can demonstrate the student's ability to appreciate the differing perspectives of classmates. Exposure to multiple cases, and the need to justify one's perspective, can help develop a diverse understanding of the theory. However, competition for airtime, especially in a large class, may make it difficult for the student to communicate how sophisticated his or her understanding is, and shy students may be especially reticent in sharing their level of understanding.

While participation has the significant strength of being continuous and timely, it can be difficult to track in a manner that students will perceive as fair. As instructor, you should be especially careful to control the amount of speaking time given to individuals, to ask probing questions that reveal the depth of students' understanding, and to keep careful records.

Written Case Assignment

The major difference between a written case assignment and a case exam is the element of time. Assignments usually have to be submitted by a set deadline, but the students typically have several weeks to complete them. Case assignments can be given to individuals or to groups.

With written assignments, you have more opportunity to set complex tasks for students that use a repertoire of skills; the longer time horizon also allows them to respond by developing a rich analysis of the situation. Of course, extended time may not be realistic: in medicine, patient visits do not last several weeks; in business, decisions must often be taken rapidly; and in law, many decisions need to be made quickly, for example, when counsel is asked questions by a judge. The extended time may be a luxury not afforded to professionals in the field.

Feedback on written assignments can be given against clear criteria, and, if the student completes several such assignments over the course of a term or year, he or she has the opportunity to improve. Student performance can also be compared against exemplars, in the form of other student reports (with their permission) or reports on cases from previous years. On the downside, feedback is not instantaneous.

To a greater extent than exams, written assignments provide students with the opportunity to think; this means they can demonstrate highly sophisticated understanding of the subject matter. By conducting multiple assignments, students can also develop and demonstrate diverse knowledge. Where written assignments are individual, students lose the benefit of comparing their perspective with others'; group assignments, on the other hand, can be compromised by dysfunction within the group.

Written assignments therefore have the potential advantage of affording the student the opportunity to think and to demonstrate a rich understanding of the theory. So that students can have an opportunity to develop their skills based on feedback, multiple assignments in a course are preferable to a single major one.

Conclusions

The type of evaluation you choose depends on your goals for the course, your own time constraints, and your group of students. However, the foregoing discussion leads us to some general suggestions for good practice in student evaluation in case courses.

Evaluate Real-World Application of Theories. In a case course, students learn to discuss ideas in the context of their application. Evaluation methods should also reflect this authentic approach, so case exams, participation, and case assignments are all legitimate evaluation methods. However, pure theory exams divorced from context would not be appropriate.

Use Diverse Methods. No evaluation method is perfect but each has its own strengths. To some extent, these are complementary, so we recommend using a variety of evaluation methods.

Use Frequent, Smaller Assignments as Well as Bigger Ones. While students have the opportunity to demonstrate sophisticated understanding in major assignments, shorter, more frequent ones provide the opportunity for continuous feedback and self-improvement.

Students Develop Self-Knowledge by Being Exposed to Others' Perspectives. The process of case discussion and feedback allows students to relate their perspective on a case to that of other students, and therefore to better understand their own biases.

Use Group Assignments to Broaden Perspectives. It follows from the preceding point that group assignments have the advantage of broadening students' perspectives. Group conflicts can arise and it is important to stay aware of how the groups are functioning.

Relate Feedback to Student's Goals. Feedback should be descriptive rather than evaluative and relate the student's efforts to achieve his or her learning goals.

Provide Clear Criteria/Exemplars. Since many cases have no single 'right' answer, students need to understand the criteria against which they are being evaluated.

Provide Multiple Opportunities to Participate. Participation in case courses requires students to prepare carefully and justify their perspective in relation to that of other students. However, students may not be able to reveal the true depth of their understanding in a free-for-all discussion in class. Other means of participation, such as online discussion groups or in-class presentations, can provide them with the opportunity to demonstrate their understanding.

12. Effective Implementation

This chapter of the guide reviews nine of the common concerns about the adoption of the case method. Sometimes students voice these concerns, and sometimes instructors raise them when considering the advisability of adopting a case method approach in their classes. For each concern, possible solutions are proposed.

1. Classes are an inefficient use of time

Instructors and students may echo this complaint about the case method. Students sometimes feel frustrated with the case method and demand that you "deliver the goods." They relate to the case method as though the instructor is deliberately obscuring the answer. Instructors who are used to a lecture method may similarly find that they need to sacrifice some content for the process of the case method. This can be frustrating, particularly where interesting material is 'lost' or other skills seen to be important are not emphasized.

Suggested Solutions

Consider the objectives of using the case method. This concern with the case method reflects a misunderstanding of the objectives of the method. The objectives of case teaching, as discussed in Chapter 5, place the process of learning on equal footing with the substance to be learned. Students continue to learn a significant amount of information in case-based courses, but in addition to that knowledge they develop critical thinking and reasoning skills. Devoting time to the development of these skills inevitably results in the loss of some substantive material. The case method may not be appropriate if its strengths do not outweigh the loss of this material.

Consider a blend of approaches. If the particular course you are teaching has minimum content or skills requirements that are highly demanding of class time, you may adopt a hybrid approach. Consider using text-based reading for some parts of the course, and case-based materials for other topics. Some of the class could be taught using the case method and other parts could require students to complete lab work. This approach may provide an appropriate balance between covering a set amount of material and skill sets and ensuring that students develop some of the skills facilitated by the case method. See the discussion in Chapter 10.

Explain the value of the case method to students. When students complain that they "just want the answer" to the case, it reflects their failure to grasp the nature of case-based learning. As set out above, one of the main purposes of using cases is to develop some of the skills required to resolve complicated real-life problems. Students need to understand the goals of the case method before they will appreciate that, many times, the 'answer' is not the central lesson from the case. You can assist students by explaining the purposes and objectives of the case method and by ensuring that your methods of student assessment evaluate not only the answer but also the students' reasoning processes.

2. Classes require too much preparatory work

One of the common concerns with the case method is that it requires too much preparatory work. This may be a concern both for instructors and students and is reflected, from instructors' perspective, in concerns among STLHE members about under-preparation by students. It is not uncommon for instructors to remark that, by the mid-term, students arrive for class without being prepared to discuss the details and possible solutions to a case.

Similarly, case teaching requires a significant amount of preparatory work on the part of instructors. If you have not prepared adequate or appropriate questions before entering the classroom, discussions can flag and lack energy or students can feel lost.

Suggested Solutions

Make workload requirements clear. Sometimes students, particularly those who are new to the case method, underestimate the degree to which case-based classes rely on preparation and participation. It helps to set out the preparation requirements of the course as part of the initial expectations for student participation—in the introductory lecture and/or in the course syllabus. It also helps to provide students with an outline of the course that clearly indicates on which day particular cases will be discussed and to remind students at the end of each class of the requirements for the subsequent class.

It is important to be clear about the information you, as the instructor, intend to provide students during the class discussion. The less direction you provide, the greater the pre-class preparation requires of students. It makes sense to directly address with the class your role as instructor. If you intend to play a largely facilitative role, students will learn that they cannot wait for answers from you. On the other hand, if you play a more directorial role, then students will come to expect that direction from you. It is inevitably frustrating for both students and the instructor if you have largely directed the class on the cases under review, and then suddenly expect students to be able to direct the discussion of the case unaided.

Emphasize the importance of preparation. There are a variety of techniques for rewarding preparation in the classroom. One of the most common ways is simply to allocate some percentage of the students' overall grade in the course to preparation and participation. This evaluation may be as simple as keeping track of which students ask questions or respond to questions in the class. There are, however, a multitude of other options for evaluating participation and preparation including requiring students to submit short notes about the case before the class begins, requiring students to post comments on the cases to an on-line class bulletin board a set number of times during the term, or providing students with a grade based on the quality of their comments in class. As discussed in Chapter 11, participation is a valid means of assessing students but it can be tricky to administer. If you do not wish to grade students on participation, you may recognize it in other ways, as discussed below.

You should model the preparation you expect in students. Begin and finish classes on time, have well-organized and prepared class notes, have prepared questions that will spark debate and discussion on the relevant points, and use technology and board-work efficiently and effectively. No one is perfect, but the more prepared you are, the more likely it is that students will be prepared.

Consider whether expectations are reasonable. A thorough analysis of a case can take a lot of time, particularly if the material in the case is new, or the case is particularly complicated. The amount of time required to fully explore a case may be surprising for instructors who have not used the case method before. It is important to leave enough class time for a thorough discussion. If too many cases are assigned for a particular class, it will be difficult and perhaps disheartening for both students and the instructor who may be inadequately prepared.

3. Students do not participate or a small group of students participates too much

In a diverse group of students, some may inevitably have more experience than others, may be familiar with the specific case, or simply be less shy than others. Encouraging broadly-based participation from students is a persistent challenge in case teaching.

It is also not uncommon for students to be keen and prepared for the first few weeks of class, but then to stop preparing and volunteering as the term wears on and good intentions fall by the wayside. This can leave a few students doing all the talking. The degree to which you are concerned about waning participation will, of course, vary based on the degree to which you teach the course in a lecture format versus a discussion format. Where you are looking for discussion and active participation, this drop in participation can be exasperating.

Suggested Solutions

Increase your tolerance for silence. Instructors often leave only a short period of time for students to think after posing a question. Waiting a few minutes may result in an increased number of responses.

Introduce other forms of participation. Introducing other forms of participation is the next step on the spectrum of responses. For example, you may ask a question, and then ask students to consider the answer in groups. Under this model, students have a chance to discuss the problem with other students—increasing their confidence and giving everyone in the class the opportunity to speak. You can then canvass the class for answers to the question.

Consider your method of questioning. Are your questions closed, leaving little room for discussion, debate, and reflection? Are the questions too difficult or too easy? Sometimes simply reframing your questions in a couple of different ways will inspire a student to answer.

Exploit student diversity. A diverse group of students offers a tremendous opportunity to have them learn from each other and build on each other's experience. On the other hand, students who are more familiar with the case or the material can dominate the discussion, and leave others behind. In addition to carefully monitoring the discussion, you can set up groups composed of more- and less-experienced students, and provide them with an assignment for reporting at the end of class. In this instance, you still need to monitor the groups to ensure that more experienced members are not dominating the discussion.

Get to know one another. People tend to have better discussions when they know each other. Leave some time in the class for students to get to know each other and you. At the beginning of a course, for example, provide some personal information and ask your students to do the same. Learning students' names can go a long way to creating an environment that fosters discussion.

Provide feedback on comments made by students. Discussions in class provide an excellent opportunity to give feedback to students about their understanding of the principles at work in the cases. It is easy feedback to give because it takes so little time (compared to marking) and it is immediate. If students think that participation may result in some constructive feedback on how to improve their understanding and reasoning process, they may be more willing to participate. As noted in Chapter 11, useful feedback means helping students see how they might have achieved their own objectives more effectively.

Require mandatory participation. The most extreme response is to require some form of mandatory participation, either graded or ungraded. Some instructors adopt the Socratic method, which requires calling randomly on students for their answers to questions. Students are no longer given the choice to participate. Other instructors institute modified forms of the Socratic method—sometimes calling on students based on their seating order, or alphabetical order. Instructors may permit students to 'pass' in particular cases—for example, if the student notifies the instructor in advance, or sits in a particular row in the classroom. Some instructors find these solutions not only assist with the discussion, but are pedagogically superior to non-mandatory participation. A more thorough discussion of styles of instruction is provided in Chapter 10.

Consider whether other factors explain the silence. Sometimes factors other than a misunderstanding of the importance of participation or general unpreparedness explain why students have stopped participating. Occasionally there will be other factors—like a major test that week in another course. Students may not be engaged in the material. Perhaps the cases are too hard, or too easy? Maybe students are unable to access the cases for some reason, or are not getting the expected support from teaching assistants. Where students fail to participate, it may be worth canvassing the class for feedback on the reasons for the non-participation.

4. Students are unfairly singled out/the Socratic method is abusive

As noted above, one of the common methods of teaching using the case method involves employing the Socratic method or some modified version of that method. Students have mixed experiences with the most extreme version of the Socratic method, where the instructor calls on students randomly and requires an answer. Some students find that experience invigorating and motivating. Other students find that it leaves them feeling disempowered and discredited. There is some evidence that students experience the Socratic method differently based on their gender and culture.

Suggested Solutions

Adopt a modified Socratic method. For some instructors the value of using the Socratic method suggests that there should be no concession to student discomfort. These adherents argue that the discomfort is part of the learning process, and that being "put on the spot" is part of the skills training students require in their professions. Others may find it makes sense to adopt some modified version of the Socratic method—some suggestions are made in Chapter 10. Using a modified Socratic method may still achieve some of the method's goals (being required to think on your feet and oral advocacy practice, for example) without subjecting students to the full force of random call.

5. Classes are too disconnected from reality/Classes are too disconnected from theory

One of the advantages of the case method is that it uses materials based on real world experiences. This sometimes leads to concerns that the case method is too disconnected from theory. Given the specificity of a case, how can anything about the general theory be learned? On the opposite side of the spectrum, though, sometimes students or instructors worry that cases are too divorced from reality. These concerns arise because of the restrictive nature of cases—for cases to be digestible, facts should be selected and presented in a coherent fashion. They cannot possibly address all of the political, social, economic, and environmental factors that might affect the reasoning or outcome. Also, students study these cases in classrooms, not by seeing real clients, patients, or market actors, for example.

Suggested Solutions

Acknowledge the limitations of the case method. Cases reflect real-world situations, but cannot be a complete replacement for experience. Using the case method students learn how to reason through a problem, and learn some of the knowledge base they will need when they try to reason though problems in their lives. It is unrealistic to expect that cases be identical to experiences outside the classroom, though, and criticizing them as too removed from reality seems unfair. You should be conscious, however, not to represent cases as being identical to the experience students will have when they leave the classroom. It can be helpful to explain the differences: in business, for example, cases provide ready access to relevant information, a luxury rarely afforded to practising managers.

Try to develop or choose cases that reflect realistic situations. One of the few uniting characteristics of cases is that they are drawn, at least roughly, from real events. Choose or develop cases that are not unduly unrealistic—outrageous and unlikely facts should be avoided, or the purpose of their use should be explained. For more on choosing and developing cases see Chapter 8.

Ensure that general principles are extrapolated. Although cases are written about specific facts, they can be used to promote inductive reasoning. Part of learning to make sense of cases requires students to extrapolate from the details of the case to more general principles. Students are then asked to distinguish cases from one another based on their conclusions about the general governing principles and to predict how new cases might be resolved. You should ensure that students focus not only on the details of the particular case, but also on the broader conclusions that might be discerned from it. Also, connect the reasoning to other cases in this and other courses in the program.

6. Classes are disorganized

Students, particularly those who are used to learning in an organized lecture format, generally raise this complaint about the case method. When students are invited to delve into the facts of the case, exploring its nuances in an attempt to discern the relevant facts and the effect of those facts on the outcome, the discussion can feel disorganized.

Suggested Solutions

Explain the class format. Some case method instructors leave their class time relatively unstructured, providing limited feedback and direction. Where this choice is made, the pedagogical explanation for that approach should be provided to students. This may not quell the students' discomfort with the feeling that there are no right answers, or that right answers are not being provided, but it may at least explain why you are conducting largely exploratory, discussion-based classes.

Provide some structure for the class. In many cases, particularly where students are unfamiliar with the case method, it may be appropriate to have a structured class discussion. Instructors might give some structure, at a minimum, to the beginning and the end of each class. For example, a professor may begin each class by summarizing some of the important points raised in the previous lecture and end the class by asking some questions about the cases to be discussed in the next lecture. The middle of the class can then be left to a relatively undirected discussion of the case without too many complaints that the class seems unwieldy. It may make sense to organize this middle section into a tightly controlled discussion as well—often through the preparation of questions, or by setting up student presentations on aspects of the case and so on.

Use your technology effectively. If you are using PowerPoint, blackboards, wipeboards, flipcharts and so on, make sure that you are using these tools in an organized way. Disorganized note taking, or note taking that does not reflect the relationship between points being made can be disorienting. When you use technology, consider how it can clarify or aid in the discussion at hand. As noted earlier, many instructors plan the layout of their board in advance of class.

7. Evaluation does not reflect the emphasis in the classroom

It is important for students to be evaluated on the material and skills that are emphasized in class. Even though this seems intuitive, a surprising number of instructors fail to evaluate on the skills and material emphasized in the classroom. For example, it is not unusual for an instructor to present a series of cases each of which addresses a discrete principle in a discipline and then to expect students to put all of those pieces together on their own in analyzing a 'monster case' for grades at the end of the term. Similarly, instructors often emphasize the process of analyzing a case in class, and then test only on the 'outcomes' of cases on the exam, without suitable reward for the reasoning process.

For suggestions on this topic, see the discussion on evaluation techniques in Chapter 11.

8. Classes encourage positional argumentation instead of consensus building

Some instructors worry that the case method encourages students to take positions without backing down at the expense of encouraging teamwork and consensus building. Often discussions will become heated in the classroom, and participants may develop dignity stakes in maintaining their position despite opposing arguments. In some circumstances this result may prove useful because the case method may teach the ability to re-cast and strengthen arguments in the face of opposition. In other cases, the class would be more effective if the participants could come to a consensus on how to proceed.

Suggested Solutions

Develop non-positional exercises. If the classroom has become positional, it may make sense to develop different exercises for students. Instead of always having a full class discussion with the aim of exposing all viewpoints and perspectives, have students discuss the case in groups. Require the groups to come to a consensus on how they would resolve the case. Discuss effective means for consensus building and team functioning as part of this exercise. As another option, when a student articulates a position, ask the student to make the best argument against his or her position as well.

9. Case information and analysis are readily available online

When cases are being used for assessment purposes, online plagiarism can be a major concern. Other instructors have used many cases and their notes are often posted on the

Internet. While this has been a concern primarily for hand-in assignments in which the student has the opportunity to search the Internet, it is increasingly becoming a concern in exam situations where a wireless network exists.

A related problem is the appropriate level of boundaries on student analysis. Students are often keen to bring to class information they have downloaded from the web or other sources. While this may enhance the learning from the case, it can be a complicating factor. The critical issues may have been resolved since the case was written by other means and the intended lessons might be diluted or even contradicted by students' further research.

Suggested Solutions

Use detection software. Software packages such as Turnitin (**www.turnitin.com**) indicate whether the material submitted has been copied from online sources. It is preferable to use this as a way of discouraging cheating rather than catching students. The use of this type of software should therefore be announced to students either in the syllabus or in class before the assignment is given.

Set clear limits on information sources. One approach is to ask the students to focus exclusively on the facts presented in the case, perhaps in conjunction with some theoretical readings. However, this is difficult to apply if the case is an old one. An alternative is to use newer cases only, so there is less time for information about them to build up on the Internet. Alternatively, you can allow students to conduct research outside the case; in this situation, you need to be thoroughly familiar not just with the case itself but with other available material and to be prepared to adjust your class or grading plan accordingly. Whichever approach you choose, you should make the boundaries clear to students.

Concluding Remarks

In this Green Guide we have attempted to provide an introduction to some of the richness the case method can bring to the classroom, regardless of the discipline. As teachers who have been able to use cases in our classes, we have been convinced of their usefulness. Cases inspire students, result in deep learning, bring context explicitly into the class, permit students to develop professional skills, allow theory to be emphasized, and raise classroom engagement.

Of course, as we acknowledge in this guide, cases might not be appropriate in every instance. For example, students may not be mature enough to prepare for class, or a set amount of material may have to be covered in a particular course.

We have also tried to address some of the difficulties that might arise when cases are used. Lack of participation, a high level of preparation, dominance by some members of the class, and the perception of disorganization, for example, have been cited as some of the issues that confront case teachers. However, we suggest that these problems can be overcome.

As we stated in the preface to this guide, cases mean different things to different people. One of the greatest assets of case teaching is its flexibility in application, and yet its constant attachment to the real world. We hope that after reading this guide you will feel better positioned to bring some of the richness cases can provide into your own teaching.

Appendix 1

Text of Memo Sent to Society for Teaching and Learning in Higher Education (STLHE) ListServ.

Cases are becoming an increasingly important teaching tool across a wide range of disciplines. They have long been established in Business, Law and Health Sciences, but have also emerged in diverse fields such as Aviation, Economics, Education and Engineering.

We are writing a Green Guide on Teaching with Cases, and would like to report on the experience of STLHE members and build on it in our discussion. We are interested in anything you have to share about teaching with cases–good, bad, or even ugly; we plan to summarize the responses and include them in the Guide.

We'd appreciate your thoughts on any or all of the following issues:

- Types of cases you select and why
- What you take into account in looking for in a case
- What you think makes a good case
- What your students think makes a good case
- How you prepare a case class
- Your keys to effective class discussion
- Ways in which you encourage student participation
- How you assess students' learning
- Difficulties you've encountered in case teaching and how you've resolved them (or not!)

Please also let us know your **field of study** so that we can get a sense of the context in which you are using cases.

Please reply to us directly, at **dunne@rotman.utoronto.ca**. Once the responses are in, we'll provide you with a summary and some of our thoughts on what it all means. Watch out for the Green Guide in the near future, which will have a full discussion of this and other issues related to case teaching!

Thanks for your help!

Kim Brooks, David Dunne, and Ros Woodhouse

References

Applegate, L. M. (1988). *Case teaching at the Harvard Business School: Some advice for new faculty* (note 9-189-062). Cambridge, MA: Harvard Business School.

Barrows, H. S. (1985). *How to design a problem-based curriculum for the pre-clinical years.* New York: Springer.

Chew, F. S. (2001). The case-based radiology teaching conference for residents: Beneficial effect of previewing cases and using answer sheets. *Academic Radiology, 8,* 993-997.

Corey, E. R. (1998). *A note on case learning* (note 9-899-105). Cambridge, MA: Harvard Business School.

Erskine, J. A., Leenders, M.R. & Mauffette-Leenders, L.A. (1998). *Teaching with cases.* London, ON: Richard Ivey School of Business.

Friedland, S. I. (1996) How we teach: A survey of teaching techniques in American law schools. *Seattle University Law Review 20* (1).

Garner, D. (2000). The continuing vitality of the case method in the twenty-first century. *Brigham Young University Education and Law Journal, 2000* (2), 307-345.

Kissam, P. (2001). The ideology of the case method/final examination law school. *University of Cincinnati Law Review (70),* 137-189.

Kleinfeld, J. (1992). Learning to think like a teacher: The study of cases. In J. H.Shulman (Ed.), *Case methods in teacher education* (pp. 33-49). New York: Teachers College Press.

Knapper, C. K. & Cropley, A. J. (1991). *Lifelong learning and higher education.* 2nd edition. London: Kogan Page.

Kolb, D.A. (1984). *Experiential learning.* Experience as the source of learning and development. Englewood Cliffs, NJ: Prentice-Hall, Inc.

Kreber, C. (2001). Learning experientially through case studies? A conceptual analysis. *Teaching in Higher Education, 6*(2), 217-228.

Kronman, A. (2000) The Socratic method and the development of the moral imagination. *University of Toledo Law Review 31*(4), 645.

Lynn, L. E. Jr. (1999). *Teaching and learning with cases: A guidebook.* New York: Seven Bridges Press.

Maufette-Leenders, L.A., Erskine, J.A. & Leenders, M.R. (1997). *Learning with cases.* London, ON: Richard Ivey School of Business.

McNair, M. P. (1954). *The case method at the Harvard Business School.* New York: McGraw-Hill.

Merseth, K. K. (1994). *Cases, case methods and the professional development of educators.* ERIC Digest. Washington, D.C.: ERIC Clearinghouse on Teaching and Teacher Education.

Searle, N. S., Haidet, P., Kelly, P. A., Schneider, V., Seidel, C. L. & Richards, B. F. (2003). Team learning in medical education: Initial experiences at 10 institutions. *Academic Medicine, 78*(10) (Supplement), S55-S58.

Shulman, J. H. (1992). *Case methods in teacher education.* (pp. 1-30). New York: Teachers College Press.

Weaver, R.L. (1991) Langdell's legacy: Living with the case method. *Villanova Law Review 36,* 517-596.

Wiggins, G. (1998). *Educative assessment: Designing assessments to inform and improve student performance.* San Francisco: Josey-Bass.

Selected Further Reading

Barnes, L. B., Christensen, C.R. & and Hansen, A.J. (1994). *Teaching and the case method.* Boston, MA: Harvard Business School Publishing.

Corey, E. R. (1980). *Case method teaching* (note 9-581-058). Boston, MA: Harvard Business School Publishing.

Cox, K. (2001). Stories as case knowledge: Case knowledge as stories. *Medical Education, 35,* 862-66.

Desiraju, R. & Gopinath C. (2001). Encouraging participation in case discussions: A comparison of the MICA and Harvard case methods. *Journal of Management Education, 25* (4) (August) 394-408.

Dooley, A. R., & Skinner, W. (1997). Casing casemethod methods. *The Academy of Management Review, 2* (2), 277—289.

Hawthorne, E. M. (1991). Case study and critical thinking. *Issues and Inquiry in College Learning and Teaching, 60.*

Garvin, D. A. (2003) Making the case: Professional education for the world of practice. *Harvard Magazine, 106,* Sept.-Oct., 1.

Golich, V. L., Boyer, M., Franco, P. & Lamy, S. n.d. *The ABC's of case teaching.* Pew Case Studies in International Affairs. Georgetown University: Institute for the Study of Diplomacy, Edmund A. Walsh School of Foreign Service.

Gragg, C. I. (1940). Because wisdom can't be told. *Harvard Alumni Bulletin,* October.

Griffith, W. (1999). The reflecting team as an alternative case teaching model: A narrative, conversational approach. *Management Learning, 30*(3), 343-62.

Herreid, C. F. (1997). What makes a good case? *Journal of College Science Teaching* (Dec/Jan), 163-65.

Kerr, O. S. (1999). The decline of the Socratic method at Harvard *Nebraska Law Review, 78,* 113.

Linder, J. (1990). Writing cases: Tips and pointers (note # 9-391-026). Boston, MA: Harvard Business School Publishing.

Lundberg, C. C., Rainsford, P., Shay. J.P., & Young, C.A. (2001). Case writing reconsidered. *Journal of Management Education, 25 (4),* 450-63.

Moskovitz, M. (1992). Beyond the case method: It's time to teach with problems. *Journal of Legal Education, 42,* 241.

Naumes, W. &. Naumes, M.J. (1999). *The art and craft of case writing.* Thousand Oaks, CA: Sage Publications.

Reynolds, J. I. (1978). There's method in cases. *The Academy of Management Review, 3* (1), 129-33.

Rangan, V. K. (1996). *Choreographing a case class* (note # 9-595-074). Boston, MA: Harvard Business School Publishing

Robyn, D. (1986). *What makes a good case?* (document N15-86-673.0). Boston, MA: Harvard University, Kennedy School of Government Case Program

About STLHE

A Message from Julia Christensen Hughes, President

The Society for Teaching and Learning in Higher Education (STLHE) is a national association of academics interested in the improvement of teaching and learning in higher education. STLHE has four primary strategic directions:

- Advancing the scholarship of teaching
- Advocating for excellence in teaching and learning
- Achieving inclusivity in all our activities
- Alliances – supporting the formation of strategic partnerships

In pursuit of these four strategic directions, the Society presents an annual conference co-hosted by a different Canadian university each year. The conference is renowned for its practical and interactive approach; attendees include university and college administrators, faculty, educational developers, and graduate students. STLHE also coordinates the country's most prestigious national teaching awards programs: the 3M Teaching Fellowships, co-sponsored by 3M Canada, in recognition of teaching excellence and educational leadership and the Alan Blizzard Award, co-sponsored by McGraw Hill Ryerson, Canada in recognition of excellence in collaborative projects that improve student learning. In addition, the Society produces the Green Guide Series—publications which address the most common challenges faculty encounter in their teaching practice.

To keep its members informed, STLHE produces a bi-annual newsletter, Teaching and Learning in Higher Education and hosts an extremely active listserv—the Forum for Teaching & Learning in Higher Education [STLHE-L@LISTSERV.UNB.CA]. Listserv members are faculty and educational developers from post-secondary institutions across Canada and beyond.

STLHE is organized by a Steering Committee, an enthusiastic group of faculty and educational developers who have either been elected by their peers or appointed in recognition of the essential role they play in supporting the Society's work.

Elected positions include a president, past president and regional representatives from: Newfoundland-New Brunswick-Prince Edward Island; Nova Scotia; Francophone Québec; Anglophone Quebec; Ontario South-West; Ontario North-East; Ontario Central; Manitoba-Saskatchewan; Alberta; and British Columbia.

In addition to these elected positions, the Chairs of the 3M Teaching Fellows Council and Educational Developers Caucus—two very important groups that are officially constituted within STLHE—serve on the Steering Committee, along with the Program Coordinator for the 3M Teaching Fellows Program, Chair of our Publications Committee, and Treasurer.

STLHE Membership

If you are interested in a forum for the exchange of ideas and information on post-secondary teaching and learning; if you believe that teaching is important and that dedication to its improvement should be recognized; if you feel that the road to professional improvement is best walked in the company of enthusiastic peers; then you should join the Society.

Membership is open to anyone who supports the aims of the Society. Information on membership dues and other matters can be obtained from the Society.

Julia Christensen Hughes (jchriste@uoguelph.ca)
C/O Teaching Support Services
University of Guelph
Guelph, Ontario N1G 2W1
web: www.tss.uoguelph.ca/stlhe/

Ordering Green Guides
To order please contact

Dalhousie University Bookstore
6136 University Ave
Halifax NS B3H 4J2
Ph: (902) 494.6704
Fx: (902) 494.3863
Email: bookstore@dal.ca
Web: www.dal.ca/bookstore

or

Centre for Learning & Teaching
Dalhousie University
Halifax NS B3H 4R2
Ph: (902) 494.1622
Fx: (902) 494.3767
Email: clt@dal.ca
web: www.dal.ca/clt